P9-BVM-349

Intelligent teaching

Intelligent Teaching

This expert, sympathetically-written introduction to acquiring and assessing teaching skills is intended as a practical guide. It is designed particularly for students of education and also for tutors and experienced teachers supervising student teaching practice.

Professor McFarland looks in detail at the immediate problems facing the young teacher: adapting to particular schools, defining objectives, maintaining discipline, deploying learning resources, and motivating learners. At the same time he relates the immediately practical to wider educational principles and newer techniques, and the book as a whole provides a systematic basis for a critical approach to teaching.

By the same author:

Human Learning

Psychological theory and educational practice

Intelligent teaching

Professional skills for student teachers

H S N McFarland
Professor of Education, University of Durham

The Author

H. S. N. McFarland read English
Language and Literature at the
University of Aberdeen, and went on
to postgraduate studies in Education
and Psychology at Edinburgh. He has
held lecturing posts at the
Universities of Edinburgh, Leeds and
St Andrews, and is now Professor of
Education at the University of Durham.
He is the author of *Psychology and
Teaching; Human Learning, a
Developmental Analysis;* and *Psychological
Theory and Educational Practice.*

Routledge & Kegan Paul
London and Boston

CARNEGIE LIBRARY
LIVINGSTONE COLLEGE
SALISBURY, N. C. 28144

First published 1973
by Routledge & Kegan Paul Ltd
Broadway House, 68–74 Carter Lane,
London EC4V 5EL and
9 Park Street,
Boston, Mass. 02108, U.S.A.
Printed in Great Britain by
Western Printing Services Ltd, Bristol
© H.S.N. McFarland 1973
No part of this book may be reproduced in
any form without permission from the
publisher, except for the quotation of brief
passages in criticism

ISBN 0 7100 7508 1 (c)
ISBN 0 7100 7515 4 (p)

Library of Congress Catalog Card Number 72–90012

371.102
m 143

Contents

91171

Preface:
people, resources,
techniques

This book is a practical guide to teaching for student teachers and, viewed in a different perspective, for all those regular teachers and tutors responsible for supervising their work. It is practical in the sense that it has much to say about ways of simply coping with some of the first teaching situations that face a young teacher. But it is practical also in the sense of providing a fairly systematic basis for a critical approach to teaching.

Trainers are bound to concern themselves with techniques and there have been great technical advances in teaching. One thinks of language teaching methods, the change from traditional class teaching to individual and small group teaching, the use of television and out-of-school visiting, the gradual spread of a less authoritarian (one hopes not less authoritative) language and manner among teachers, the introduction of at least some forms of examination more sensibly related to the actual work of schools, and the development of more varied learning materials or resources for specific purposes. However, while these technical improvements should in no way be deprecated, one often feels that the most powerful resources, for good or ill, are the general physical and social character of the region in which a pupil lives, the structures and attitudes that prevail in the individual school, and the personal and general character of the individual teacher.

There is later reference to the encyclopaedic and apostolic urges in education. The terms are used in a wide sense—the first to denote all those efforts to educate people by ingenious summaries and systems, the second to denote the persistent search for inspiring persons whose discipleship will somehow bring educational salvation. Encyclopaedism is rationalistic and orderly. Apostolicism is content that the divine wind bloweth where it listeth. Each has its appeal and yet also its deception. They represent the tension between resources and persons—a theme perennially relevant to teaching.

Anyone who teaches is at least a tacit educational theorist. Since teachers are not particularly characterized by taciturnity, most of them express views on education from time to time and become explicit theorists. Theory, however is a *bête noire* for many. This problem is analysed in the last chapter. Briefly, it seems likely that the practical contribution of theory to teaching is as a means of sustaining the spirit and means of self-criticism, so that teachers can be professionally autonomous rather than pedagogical robots. The beginner will always and inescapably have to face the tension between self-construction and self-criticism as a teacher. The first should predominate, but the second must also have a place. The conventional plea to make theory more practically relevant is understandable, but partly misconceives the relationship between theory and practice.

One of the most difficult teaching skills is that of sustaining a balanced perspective on education. There are so many people charging off in so many different directions. Some do not want 'to be tied down'. One knows what they mean, but people have to tie themselves down to something, at least provisionally. Some believe 'things change so fast' that today's attitudes and skills will be useless tomorrow. There is indeed much fast change, but much does not change fundamentally, some things that do change become worse instead of better, and there is a *reductio ad absurdum* if change is thought to outrun education at such a pace that education must be abandoned completely.

Some constantly remind us that 'situations vary so much' or that 'everyone has his own prejudices', as if this meant that all rational discussion was futile or at least relatively unimportant. Discussion can be tilted too much towards a narrow rationalism, or a narrow emotivism, but there are objectivities and stabilities amid the complex motions of the educational tides, and these are as important as the elusive individual waves that shatter themselves on particular beaches.

Some raise tantalizing banners with words on them like The Child, The Teacher, The Subject, Integration, Rationalization, Initiation, or Compensation. But no slogan can be a substitute for a balanced and justified educational policy. Falsely contrasted stereotypes are no substitute for an authentic view of teaching practice that relates defensible objectives and reasonably well attested resources and techniques to the particular problems of each situation in which the teacher exercises his personal responsibility for interpretation and implementation.

In trying to interpret the problems of teaching practice the author has been indebted to many people. The bibliography at the end charts one's most direct indebtedness to other writers—sometimes all the greater when they provoke partial disagreement. Students and colleagues on whom one tries out conjectures have supplied what Paulsen (1906), talking about lectures, called the salutary 'opposition of the hearer who is repelled by artificiality and sophistry'. The same colleagues have also provided the positive stimulus and example of their own teaching and concern with teaching.

As always, one is especially indebted to one's wife for frank criticism and loving encouragement, and to one's secretary, Mrs Maureen Chrystal, for cheerfully translating scribble into type.

Teaching practice: some fundamentals

Teaching: a practical and intelligent approach

Two main ideas underline the discussion of teaching practice in this book. One is the truism that teaching skills are acquired and developed by both practice and reflection, and that this process is continuous from the student teacher gaining his initiation, to the mature teacher setting himself new and more sophisticated teaching objectives. The second is that one can explore the main general problems of teaching practice in a way that will help individuals to think and act more intelligently in relation to their own specific teaching practice.

The either–or approach to practice and reflection is stupid. Putting practice on a pedestal encourages complacent adaptation to what happens to prevail at a particular time and place. Putting reflection on a pedestal (probably labelled 'theory', in the opprobrious sense of that much maligned term) leads to a hypothetical universe that drifts further and further away from things as they are. Practice and reflection are mutually dependent and corrective. The importance of recognizing the full force of this is increased by two major current trends. One is the trend towards more massive innovation in educational systems. The other is the trend towards increasing the explicit responsibility of all experienced teachers for the professional initiation of beginning teachers.

A book like this obviously cannot *be* a teaching practice, but its objective is to look in an analytic and practical way (1) at the teaching situation as it is liable to confront the beginning teacher, (2) at several of the perennial problems of learning to teach—observation, lesson preparation, method, discipline, and assessment, and (3) at certain wider aspects of teaching practice, including its relationship to educational research and to the study of educational philosophy,

1

psychology, and sociology. The author has analysed in detail else-where (McFarland, 1971) what teaching practices and principles can and cannot be derived from the study of psychology. The present book touches briefly on how one can throw a connecting line in the other direction, from teaching practice towards the theory of educa-tion. But most of the book endeavours to keep close to practical teaching, although the means of analysis as distinct from the material to be analysed must derive from education as an analytic discipline (Education with a capital E, as it is ironically expressed).

Diversity of teaching and teachers

It would take a long time to list all that might be called teaching practice. The list would have to allow for the huge diversity of things that are taught, of ways of teaching them, of people who do the teaching, of aims that the teaching is meant to subserve, and of national communities and formal and informal institutions within which the teaching takes place.

In the widest sense any sample of teaching illustrates some teaching practice or other—the don giving his lecture, the football coach preparing his team for the Saturday match, the religious catechist testing his flock, the mother guiding her daughter's first efforts at knitting, the preacher inspiring his congregation, the lover winning the affectionate response of the beloved, the mathematics master correcting his pupil's exercises, the language laboratory tape shaping the linguist's speech, the headmaster commending or reproving conduct, the teacher or parent hearing the young child's reading. The list of specific examples could go on for ever, but even the main general forms of teaching are varied—lessons, demonstrations, lectures, discussions, programmed learning, practical exercises, rehearsing memorized material or recently acquired skills, educational visits, and all kinds of miscellaneous experience if the experience is planned with an educational end in view.

A characterization of an individual's or a country's teaching practice can be made in terms of the particular teaching processes or the particular teaching objectives that are favoured. Some countries and some schools prefer uniformity in aim and method, others prefer variety. Some teachers emphasize explicit instructional methods, others give instruction a small role but a larger one to subtle organiza-tion of individual or group experience. Traditional academic objec-tives may dominate a teaching situation, or these may be balanced (or dislodged) by new academic objectives or non-academic objectives. Different areas of knowledge and skill are given different weightings by different teachers and institutions. Similarly, different stages of an educational system may be differently valued, with some relatively neglected, others perhaps overvalued at any time.

Factors like these are of equal interest to the experienced educationist attempting to assess an educational system and to a beginning teacher attempting to assess his teaching practice school. The former has to consider a wider range and complexity of phenomena, but even one teaching practice school can also represent a wide array of historical, ideological, sociological, psychological, and administrative factors. Some of these factors will have a direct bearing on the work of a student teacher, while others at least provide a first chance of studying at first hand how teaching belongs in a wider social context.

Teaching practice in the sense mainly intended in this book is what student teachers do when they go into schools to teach groups of children for limited periods of time under the professional guidance of the regular teachers and of college or university tutors. At least that is how one might put it if it had to be put in a single sentence. It does not take much reflection to see that, in this sense too, teaching practice must really include a wide range of very different circumstances and experiences. A list of questions may suggest part of the possible range.

Is the school infant, junior, middle, or secondary? Is it urban, suburban, or rural? How many pupils and teachers does it have? Are there pupils of both sexes or only of one? What kinds of social background do the pupils have and what educational considerations ensue? Is the school controlled by a religious denomination or does it depend simply on a public education authority? Is it completely or partly independent? What is the balance between men and women teachers, younger and older teachers? What range of qualifications does the staff have? Of what vintage are the school buildings? What is the character of the interior and what facilities are available or lacking?

What special traditions or aspirations does the school have? What blend of authority and freedom prevails? (Sometimes a delicate question to be considered privately rather than put crudely to those sensitively involved!) Are classes constituted with a view to grouping pupils of similar general ability (streaming), or of similar ability taken subject by subject (setting), or of positively dissimilar ability? What particular children will one be called upon to teach and what is it that they will be expected to learn? Will one have some of the breadth of responsibility of a primary teacher or be concerned with teaching a specialist subject to able secondary pupils? Is it a short practice where one may be allowed to give the regular teacher a small helping hand or a longer practice where there may be a bigger opportunity of accepting full responsibility for a limited section of work? Will the emphasis be on subordination to existing routines or will the school sacrifice some of its hard-won systems to the in-experienced enthusiasms of a beginning teacher?

There can be no general answer to these questions, for teaching practice must vary with all the varying circumstances of the schools themselves and with the attitudes and personalities of the regular teachers. The only practical policy for the student teacher is to take time (1) to identify the character of his own teaching practice situation, and (2) to work out what he can best do to be helpful, and to develop the particular skills that can be exercised in that situation. There must be diversity of teaching practice because of actual diversity of circumstances and ideals. This is so even in countries where the political system imposes a large measure of educational uniformity, and has still greater force where the political system supports diversity on principle.

The consequence for the individual student is that there can be no complete or perfect teaching practice in which all teaching skills are cultivated, but only opportunities to cultivate particular sets of skills at any one time. It may be that tutors could concentrate more on identifying what sets of skills can be genuinely practised in particular settings. But it would be too pessimistic to let existing limitations exclude all idealism or hope of overcoming circumstances. And it is hardly tactful or constructive to dwell upon the limitations, however striking, of a given school rather than on its potentialities.

The inevitably wide variation in the meaning of teaching practice is not just a question of chance. It is not something that happens to be the case now but might not be in the future. Part of the variation may be of this fortuitous character, but a great deal of it is bound to persist, whatever is done. Physical resources and human attitudes cannot be transformed totally and instantaneously, even if this were desirable, which it probably is not. As resources and attitudes catch up with one set of ideals, new ideals are already being formulated and propagated.

Equally fundamental is the consideration that the concept of teaching is bound to embrace a very wide set of ideals and techniques, some of which may overlap only partly or hardly at all. What does university lecturing in mathematics have in common with the socializing aspect of infant school teaching; teaching Latin to the top set in an independent school with teaching the practical conduct of life to a class of early school leavers with no academic bent; or the teaching of the mechanics of reading to some seven-year-old slow learners with teaching literary criticism to students specializing in literature? It would be a quite entertaining exercise to identify the common elements, but they would have to be formulated in elusively general terms. It is the differences of goal and relevant technique that stand out in all their particularity.

The inescapable diversity of teaching has sometimes been obscured by the wish that all kinds of teacher and teaching should be equally esteemed, and that such equal esteem should be marked by equal material rewards. All good teaching should, of course, be highly esteemed, but the controversy about esteem and reward is complex and not directly relevant to the present theme of teaching practice, except in so far as it sometimes seems to suggest, perhaps unintentionally, that there is some single pattern which defines good teaching or the good teacher. This would pose a problem for beginning teachers, for, if anything is as diverse as the range of tasks that may be called teaching, it is the range of people who hope to call themselves teachers. Good teaching must mean the kind of teaching that is specifically related to the task in hand. And the good teacher must be the teacher who brings *his* potentialities (not some set of hypothetical potentialities) relevantly to bear on *his* teaching task. This does not mean that any teacher is as good as another, for some have wider abilities and potentialities, but it means, particularly for the beginner, that the only practical policy is to concentrate on what one can oneself hope to do in the circumstances, and not on what someone else might do, or what might be done in radically different circumstances.

Learning on the job

The argument just outlined might seem so relativistic that one had better say no more about teaching practice, for what generalizations can be made about such a chameleon topic? Would not each teacher, or at least each category of teacher, require his own guide to teaching practice? In one sense this is true, but specific guidance can be given only by tutors and regular teachers helping the beginner on the spot. The value of such guidance is widely appreciated by student teachers. They feel that what is done in school is the real thing, and, while teachers and tutors naturally vary in the usefulness of their specific guidance, at least they are attempting to provide it and not just detached general advice.

The word 'apprenticeship' sometimes comes into play at this point, with its suggestion of practical learning on the job under expert practitioners. It is attractive as an ideal, although potentially deceptive too in begging the questions of whether being on site necessarily guarantees any practical learning, of whether any practical learning that takes place is of the best kind in terms of the means employed and the ends pursued, and of what the scope of the expert practitioner's expertise is—again in terms of both means and ends. The real thing may be either the right or the wrong thing.

Despite this caveat, there is a second argument in favour of learning on the job rather than by reading books or listening to general analysis and advice. It has to do with the amount of advice that a person can digest and apply. Some people are impressively quick in discriminating the key aspects of a problem. They have learned to ignore the subsidiary and incidental points and to see those that matter—those that make most difference. Others at the opposite extreme never seem to be able to see the wood for the trees. They seem to treat everything as of equal importance without discrimination. Most people are not at either of these extremes, but at some point in between. Moreover, while some may be brilliant or dull at most things, most people vary from one kind of problem to another, depending on the specific skills and experience they have acquired.

The student teacher is challenged to perform two sets of very difficult discriminations. He has to try to digest intellectually quite complex sets of ideas about educational aims and processes—an area of study which is fascinating, but intrinsically complex, partly because it must be concerned with different kinds of knowledge (the social sciences, philosophy, the diverse subjects taught in schools), partly because some of these kinds of knowledge are permanently open and controversial in nature (competing value systems, competing interpretations of the actual nature of man or society). Then, as he tries to make sense of that, he must also discriminate what particular steps he must take to get a specific group of children to acquire definite skills, attitudes, or knowledge. And here it is not just a demand for intellectual discrimination but for the complete practical implementation of a small-scale teaching plan, confronted by the refractory challenge of children in all their variety, possibly by the expert appraisal of a teacher or tutor, and, of course, by the self-appraisal through which we all try to justify our past efforts or revise our ideas about future endeavours.

The account just given probably makes things sound more complex than they usually are, but it highlights the psychological fact that people tend to seek some means of simplification. Emphasis on the advantage of school practice or experience over books or lectures can be one form of this simplification. Practice seems to pose enough problems of its own without adding those of what is loosely called theory. A clear conception of aims and appropriate methods may seem logically prior to any attempt at rational teaching in a school, but it may also seem easier to plunge into the practical situation and hope that something can be made of it, even if one is not sure what that something will be. Those who insist on the importance of first considering aims sometimes perform their own simplification by reducing what are intrinsically complex and controversial problems to a set of formulae, dressed up in a semblance of theoretical justification. No one is immune from the temptation to sweep at least some of the dust under the carpet. It is still there but you do not see it.

Regular teachers called upon to admit students to their classes may feel ambivalent attitudes towards the problem just outlined. On the one hand they may hope or expect that students will be in some sense practically prepared before they start teaching practice. On the other, they may believe that students should fit in with what the school is doing (as they must to some extent) and not upset a successful working pattern with outside plans based on different assumptions about aims or methods. There is scope here for fundamental mistakes about what is possible as well as for superficial mistakes arising from accidental failures in communication. There is no general answer to the problem, except persistent attempts to keep channels of communication open and in use.

There is a third argument (of a kind) for more practice and less theory in addition to the arguments about doing the real thing, and about simplifying the student's total situation. This is that it may be easier to assert the power of circumstances over principles when the arena is the arena of circumstances—the school classroom rather than the tutor's study. Even if the tutor is not directly challenged (which he may be), the student can still think his own thoughts or unburden them to student friends. What about the possibly conflicting advice offered by tutor and class teacher? What would the tutor really do in the same circumstances? Or, if one can imagine him probably doing better than oneself, how does that help a student whose inexperience, tender years, and trainee status pose problems that only he can fully appreciate? This can lead to the feeling not only that practice is better than theory, but that unsupervised practice would leave one freer to develop one's own skills than supervised practice. The intrusions of tutor or teacher, however friendly, carry at least a mild threat of criticism and deflation.

The desirable and the possible

What underlies the feeling about the importance of practice is the realization that having to do a job disciplines one's effort in a different way from just thinking about the job. Problems that may be imagined and worried about often do not arise at all in practice. Problems that do arise define themselves in practical detail, which poses its own difficulties but at least eliminates hypothetical speculation. However, beginning teachers themselves would rarely subscribe to any naïve idea that it was enough simply to turn up in a classroom and start teaching. The question is, what kind of preparation for teaching practice is best?

One basic part of the answer has already been suggested. The teacher must try to identify limited objectives which he has some chance of achieving with the human and physical resources genuinely at his disposal. This completely practical principle is none the less more easily stated than applied, for it takes time and effort to find out (a) what are the regular teacher's objectives in a particular situation, (b) what part of these objectives can be reasonably pursued in a given unit of teaching, (c) what the pupils' resources are in terms of abilities, habits, and specific scholastic attainments (all of these varying among individuals as well as among classes or schools), (d) what material resources are available (paper, pencils, books, illustrations, suitable spaces or surfaces, projectors that work, etc.), and (e) what one's own human resources are (particular knowledge, skills, or interests; strengths and weaknesses; deficiencies that can be speedily remedied or that require longer application; perhaps plenty of time to prepare or, on other occasions, shortage of time necessitating stricter economy and direction of effort).

Although these things are central to teaching success, there can be no question of immediately or always assessing them fully or accurately. Teaching involves a great deal of marginal coping with new and complex situations, where even 'getting by' may be a minor triumph. Where teaching follows a fairly well expected pattern it still takes time to get to know children well, to master the exploitation of physical resources, to learn what objectives are reasonable within practical circumstances, and to find out what one's own capabilities (disappointingly or surprisingly) are. What matters is to be aware of the relevance of the points outlined rather than to be unduly obsessed by trying to give them all full weight. Just knowing the points may solve few problems, but ignoring them can positively create problems. It is better to have a map of the territory, even if one's map-reading skills are unsophisticated.

Successful teaching has to do with relating the desirable and the practicable in a complex and ever-changing human situation. The dynamic nature of teaching is one of its basic features, even if some individual teachers may appear less than dynamic. A teacher may be dominated by some lofty ideal of what is desirable. His idealism may drive him to achieve what others have considered impracticable; or else practical obstacles may cause him to moderate his aims. On another occasion he may have such modest aspirations that he does not use all the potential in the teaching situation, now underreaching instead of overreaching himself. This play between the ideal and the practicable is never-ending. It is part of the meaning of teaching and requires a certain readiness to venture, but also a readiness to moderate the raptures of success and the disappointments of occasional failure.

The dynamic character of teaching does not imply that it is all a scene of turbulence and drift. Many think mistakenly that a situation is either completely understood and controlled or else is hardly understood and controlled at all. This sometimes arises from projecting temporary individual perplexity on to the entire teaching scene, or from arbitrarily spotlighting a small turbulent part of the scene, despite the scene as a whole being demonstrably stable and well ordered. The fact that turbulence has a more dramatic appeal than order tends to intensify this exaggeration of its scope and importance. The fact that the beginner has yet to master the secrets of order makes him more aware of turbulence—not particularly turbulence in the sense of pupils imperfectly controlled (although that can be a problem) but in the sense of the whole relationship between objectives and resources imperfectly controlled. Time, practice, and reflection solve most problems.

Careful consideration of a teacher's resources reminds one that some can be mustered in a short space of time (perhaps exemplifying the quality that is named resourcefulness) while others have to be built up over long periods. One may prepare a set of pupils' work cards in an evening for use next day, but one cannot in an evening learn to play the piano for the singing lesson. One may do a short private practice of chalkboard writing which shows benefits at once, but it may be a longer, more difficult job to modify a strongly established speech habit (speed, monotony, er-ing, clenched teeth, mannerisms like 'you see'). One may cook up a stimulating lesson from history, science, or any of the other major disciplines, but it takes years of private study to have any real command of such disciplines. It is practical to distinguish the different requirements necessary to acquire various teaching skills, and make sure that one does not delay the acquisition of at least a few of those that are bound to require more time. Things like musical proficiency or academic knowledge or a thorough study of learning to read are not sufficient to ensure teaching skill, but they are part of teaching skill. It is quite artificial to draw any sharp line between knowledge and skill in some subject and knowledge and skill in practical teaching techniques. The two things are distinguishable but still closely interrelated.

The problem just discussed is one aspect of the problems of time and timing which loom so large in teaching. 'If only there were more time' is the *cri de coeur* one hears from teachers at every level. Tutors who urge their students to plan lessons carefully, so that they do not overrun the time allowed, will themselves lecture up to and past the last minute of the lecture period. Students still accustomed to the dense outpourings of their lectures are knocked temporarily off balance by how little pupils can do in forty minutes. And yet, while there is this ravenous appetite for time, much of what is crammed into it has little effect, representing more the uncontrolled impetus of established systems rambling on like driverless steam-rollers. It is not easy to escape these trends, although the path of escape is clear enough in principle—do less (in one sense) in the available time, but try to do something that will make a more per-manent and desirable difference to the learners.

Teaching by objectives

The principle just stated is part of a practical schematic approach to learning that has always been implicit in educational endeavours, but has received more explicit and detailed formulation in recent times, particularly in the context of curriculum reform. The scheme (already partly adumbrated as an approach to teaching practice) amounts in its essence to the following sequence:

1 State your objectives in as specific terms as possible.

2 Note any special problems that will have to be overcome.

3 Assess what resources you will require and actually have.

4 State the programme of work that seems most likely to surmount or evade the problems and achieve the objectives with the available resources.

5 Evaluate the success of the programme, with a view to revising it or the objectives if necessary.

This scheme can be applied to large or small units of learning—to a student's work with a particular class for a whole term or a half-hour unit of work with a small group on a specific topic. Con-temporary exponents of this approach often distinguish their version from traditional versions by the emphasis on (a) the importance of formulating specific rather than general objectives (how will the learner's behaviour be altered when the learning is complete?) and (b) the importance of systematically assessing whether the objective has in fact been achieved (how has the learner's behaviour changed?). A corollary would be that all large-scale objectives must be analysed into their constituent small-scale objectives. A wider objective might be to learn to read, but is the immediate objective to distinguish 'b' from 'd', or to confirm newly acquired reading skills with a 'supple-mentary' reader that raises no fresh problems, or to help a class of students to read a complex text in a way that enables them to abstract the heart of its argument?

Another example of a wider objective might be that of the present book, to help student teachers (and possibly their mentors) to think more analytically, intelligently, and practically about teaching skill, but this must be subdivided into the subordinate objectives suggested by the chapter headings, and these into the more subordinate objectives within chapters. For each objective there should be theoretically some explicit test of whether it has been achieved. For example, anyone who continued to maintain, let us say, that all primary school teachers should receive *precisely* the same kind of teaching practice would have failed to achieve this chapter's objective of seeing why this can and should never happen.

A person who seriously maintained that teaching practice is literally the only thing that counts, would have failed to achieve the objective of seeing why practice can never be immune to possible criticism on grounds that go beyond the immediate situation. A student who could think of no reason for the failure of the school geography lesson he had carefully prepared from relevant university notes on the topic would have failed to achieve the objective of applying the diagnostic scheme outlined in this chapter. Achieving an objective in these cases might be indicated by the fact that the student could analyse a teaching problem in a manner less open to question, or by the fact that his teaching practice was clearly improved by consideration of the arguments put forward.

The practical utility of formulating precise objectives has been stated, but a note of qualification must be struck. Can human endeavours always be expressed in terms of clear objectives? And, even where they can be, is that necessarily the most desirable thing? Even the most systematic aspects of human life are blurred by the erratic, the unexpected, and the irrational. Objectives commonly emerge slowly from a surrounding confusion, with shreds of that confusion continuing to adhere to them. It is not just a question of incidental confusions. Many objectives are controversial by their very nature. While it may be rational for each person to define his own position as specifically as possible, contrary definitions by others challenge and imperil one's specifications and reasons. The practical need for compromise may itself be a legitimate objective.

Competing objectives may have to abate their sharpness to have a chance of partial achievement in a world of diverse values. Sharp objectives may have to be kept in their place to encourage new objectives which have not yet been precisely conceived. Unnecessary vagueness cannot be defended, but sharp definition is just *one* desirable feature among others which may be more important in assessing the relative value of objectives. And at least some enthusiastic exponents of precise objectives express their own objectives

glibly in terms of the approved formula, simultaneously discount-
enancing other objectives because their proponents have not mastered
the jargon. This is lifemanship in the guise of rationalism.

Recognizing limitations to the ideal of precise objectives does not
invalidate the general principle. Objectives are obviously important
in terms of trying to do what is most justifiable. This is the point at
which the study of educational philosophy impinges directly and, of
course, controversially, on teaching practice. But objectives are
practically important in another sense. A great amount of unsuccessful
teaching is due to the selection of objectives which, however admirable
in principle, are not practical for a particular situation. Some of the
major categories of mistake include aiming too high or too low for the
particular learners, giving overriding precedence to the teacher's
academic objectives when the pupil's objectives may be essentially
practical, largely excluding emotional and personal objectives when
these are in fact highly significant for academic and less academic
learners alike, or (to give an example in the opposite direction)
assiduously exhorting the pupils to be creative or imaginative when
adding to their concrete experience or training specific skills might be
a more achievable objective, and a basis for creativity in a less elusive
sense.

In teaching practice the problem of feeling for the right objective,
in the sense of the objective that is justifiable in itself and is within
conceivable practical reach of the learners, is always there. Obviously,
the more experienced teacher develops a surer sense of what is right
in his sphere, but even he may be radically challenged by a change of
circumstances or values. And, even when the challenge from outside
is not in any way special, individuals generate challenges for themselves. Even when no one else fails to admire an individual's achievement he himself may grow dissatisfied and strive towards fresh
objectives.

Rewards and challenges

The matters to be discussed in the ensuing chapters can be viewed
more practically and sharply if a word is said about the character of
educational argument. Educational problems are intrinsically diverse,
but this diversity is extended infinitely by the huge variety of people
who have an interest in education, whether in the sense of a sympathy
with particular educational problems, or in the sense of a vested
interest in using education to further limited purposes. Education is
the concern of the scholar or researcher trying to validate some
analysis of its problems in scrupulous detail, but also of the politician
canvassing particular educational policies as part of a much wider

social and political platform. It is the theme of popular journalism and scholastic ceremonies, of the well-informed and the ignorant, the unintelligent and the intelligent. And the theme changes its tone from plausible persuasion to hard propaganda, from self-indulgent rhetoric to hard, sophisticated logic, as different people take it up in different contexts.

Teaching practice is like other educational topics in being inevitably exposed to currents of vested interest and emotion as well as of cogent evidence and reasoning. That this should be so is no bad thing, for such is the mixed pattern of life itself. But it does matter that each person, and particularly the professional teacher, should learn to mark the character and context of different assertions. Is one dealing with mere slogans, or with the long but limited experience of a single individual or institution, or with a principle supported by the experience of many different people in different times and places, or with some experimental findings that may be valid within their confines but either valid or invalid beyond them, or with the relentless propaganda of a vested interest, or with the power of a great surge of public sentiment in favour of a particular practice or policy?

Experienced teachers stand by their experience, educational researchers see salvation in more funds for research, politicians subordinate education to wider political purposes. Parents want simply the best for their children, whether they consider that to mean keeping them at school as long or as short as possible. Administrators pursue the economic and orderly deployment of resources. Children are adaptable and make the best of the education that confronts them, or else devise ways of evading its influence if not its presence. Student teachers hope that they will make out all right, and, on the whole, most do.

One cannot discuss teaching practice without talking about problems, and, by definition, these are the difficult bit of the whole exercise. However, there are also encouraging features for the beginning teacher. The variety of teaching, already stressed, implies that there is hope of succeeding in some aspects even if one is not suited to others. It is only realistic to build up from strong points rather than waste time lamenting weaknesses.

A second encouraging feature is that, while existing institutions create some problems, they also solve many. Not even the experienced teacher is called upon—or, for that matter, allowed—to do the job himself. There are colleagues and curricula, books and materials, well developed methods and work programmes, children who even at their most difficult are human beings in search of sympathy and susceptible of guidance in the long run, and educational traditions (not all of them deplorable) which can support individual endeavour in subtle and powerful ways. It is not necessary, although it can be helpful, for the individual teacher to feel that he has some *vocation* for teaching—a kind of divine calling.

Nor is the term 'born teacher' more than a rhetorical device to denote a limited proportion of teachers, who may admittedly have been born with a disposition of temperament potentially relevant to teaching, but who typically have also been favoured by an upbringing which happens to have given them an early start in acquiring relevant skills—for example, in social interaction. Born teachers do not by themselves keep an education system going, even if they do give it a special leavening. A few may have a vocation or be born teachers, but the vast majority come to teaching in a more down-to-earth frame of mind. Teaching is a job at which one can earn a living (*pace* salary negotiators), develop professional skills by study, practice, and reflection, and have that satisfaction peculiar to facing the challenge of young people. It is not an all-or-nothing job, but one where even partial victories are worthwhile.

A third encouraging feature is the fact that teaching makes a substantial contribution to the social welfare of the whole community, even if one is sharply aware of how much more it might do. Plenty is said about what society needs and about the shortcomings of education in meeting them, but those who teach still represent one of the most genuine and active endeavours to give young people their cultural birthright, including initiation into the intellectual disciplines which enable people to appreciate what is good and criticize what is bad or inadequate in society. This is not meant to imply the false notion that only education matters, for it must take its place beside physical security, good homes and health, employment opportunities, and other social benefits. But education is distinctive and fundamental in its contribution to the general good, and that admittedly limited part of education which consists in teaching gives young people one real means of converting idealism into action, even if there is an inevitable partial loss of full power in the energy change.

Three encouraging features are perhaps enough if one is not to abandon the intention of keeping close to the practical. It might be best, therefore, to conclude this chapter with a short elaboration of the more challenging side of teaching—the problems that have to be solved for oneself, that are most frustrating when solutions are not found but also most rewarding when they are.

One of the most common student reactions to teaching practice is the demand for more specific, more detailed recipes for particular situations. Since each situation is unique if you take literally everything into account, the only complete recipe would be for each to do his job, neither giving nor receiving comment—a kind of flight into existentialist isolation. This is not possible—not, at any rate, if one expects to receive eventually a salary for a public service. But the idea is not utterly mad. There is a true sense in which even the beginning teacher has to enter into the partly isolating responsibility of his own teaching, where imaginative resourcefulness may be more important than tutorial advice, however wise.

One might draw an analogy with motoring. How fast should one drive? Quite simple—as fast as one wants to within the legal limits and within the bounds of accurate consideration for all of the circumstances that affect the safety and convenience of oneself and others. But what if one has an accident? Again simple—one's consideration of the circumstances must have been in some way deficient. How then should one teach? In any way that takes account of all of the circumstances relevant to the achievement of the intended objective in that situation. But what if something goes wrong? One must have failed to take account of some circumstances or of the appropriateness of the objective.

There seem to be two ways out of the circularity—in the situation, the practical acceptance of responsibility; out of the situation, an attempt with the help of an observer to agree on some of the causes of what happened, even if there must be a remnant of divergent interpretation. Actor and observer have complementary strengths and weaknesses. Whoever is teaching has the strength of his actual responsibility and involvement, the weakness of his non-detachment. The observer has the strength of detachment but the weakness of not being the one to do the teaching.

Teaching is certainly not just technique. It is partly a revelation of oneself and of others, a sophisticated exploration of intellect, personality, circumstance, and social interaction. It is the casting of bread on the waters as well as the calculating pursuit of declared objectives. Some of those who develop most authority (in the best sense) in teaching do so by losing sight of themselves and living in concern for young people. But lack of selfish concern does not mean lack of concern for one's own standards. Good standards, genuinely subscribed to, constitute a beneficial teaching influence, just as the many false pretensions of the educational world teach their powerful lesson in hypocrisy.

Teaching—like all jobs, of course—can become a relatively quiet life of accommodation to people and circumstances, a kind of death of radicalism. Both accommodation and radicalism are valuable, and one permanent feature of teacher education must be the subtle interplay between these two urges. Experienced teachers should have the confidence, as many do, to give scope for at least limited experiment by student teachers, as well as initiating them tactfully into the art of accommodation. The beginners must play their part in seeing what the human situation, and not just what their idea of teaching practice, demands.

There is a radicalism that consists in much talk about utopian change and a radicalism that consists in practical action at the roots of specific human problems. The first is dramatic and self-indulgent, the second less dramatic in superficial effect but more so in underlying achievement. Neither experienced nor beginning teachers have a monopoly of either of these radicalisms.

First practice

2

The teaching practice that comes first chronologically is often particularly stimulating. Even if there are special problems about the circumstances, there is satisfaction in getting to grips with the actual teaching of children. Indeed, students may feel partly frustrated if they have to spend too long on observation alone when they are eager for a more active role.

Some of the problems of a first practice are, of course, prime problems in a wider sense. Some are problems that continue to be conspicuous, generating a demand for practical, in the sense of immediately practicable, solutions. Some are problems that have to do with understanding a new institution and, consequently, have to be faced every time one goes to a different school. An important example of this is the case of the school in which a teacher does his first practice as a salaried probationer.

This chapter, therefore, should not be understood as dealing with first practice only in the narrowest possible sense. It is concerned with any of the problems that seem most urgent for beginners. There will not be too much emphasis on problems of class control, teaching method, or assessment, for these are sufficiently important to deserve extended discussion in subsequent chapters. Two further points should be remembered. One is that the initial complexity of teaching can be tempered in various ways, including introductory visits to schools by individuals or small groups. The other is that, while some practical problems persist, others are eventually so completely solved that a young teacher with even a little experience may have forgotten the things that seemed practical problems for him as a student.

On the threshold

Consider some of the thresholds on which the student teacher may stand—the threshold of adult and professional life, the threshold of a particular school or classroom, the threshold between ideal and achievement, between being taught and teaching, between unsalaried and salaried responsibility, between tact and hypocrisy, between student world and child world. An awareness of so many thresholds might make one hesitate to say what advice was most practical.

The apophthegms of teaching commonly have to be applied and interpreted in individual cases. Otherwise, idealism, which is so necessary even for practical purposes, may take on a comically vague aura, tempting the facile irony particularly of those hostile to, or ignorant of, the problems of educating a *whole* community. Adopt a purposive approach—but *how* and for *what* purpose? Project your own personality—but is this not really an invitation to the difficult, if not impossible, task of *changing* one's own personality? Regard each child as an individual—but what does this counsel of perfection mean in the face of forty potentially discordant individuals and a public expectation of achieving educational and social norms? Well then, think of yourself as a partner in the shared activity of learning—but the student teacher is an unpaid partner, lacking the regular teacher's established status; and the gap between the mental sophistication of student and pupil (in most cases) suggests a very unequal partnership.

These antitheses suggest a general dilemma of educational analysis—that it can veer with the greatest of ease into lack of realism at one extreme and into cynicism at the other. This dilemma may be compounded for the beginner if he fails to distinguish the requirements of analysis and the requirements of action in particular circumstances. Honest analysis follows where logic and the evidence lead. By contrast, the student teacher in particular practical circumstances is often primarily challenged (not unreasonably) to conform with a generally given pattern, while finding some corner of the pattern where he can make a small positive contribution in accordance with his own skill and conscience.

This points in the direction of conformity as a major practical principle in the first instance, even if, for a student, non-conformity (itself a form of conformity) has almost come to seem *de rigueur*. But will conformism produce teachers who can 'prepare children for a highly complex technologically based economy, in which they would be capable of coping with and generating change' (Burgess, 1971)? The question could be debated, but its present relevance is to mark out the way in which controversy is inescapable even as one tries to define what is really practical. If practical comes to mean expedient (pleasing as many people as possible—headmaster, tutor, class teacher) a charge of cynicism is invited, and the possibility of displeasing after all. If some middle-of-the-road policy is followed (a little but not too much of all the popular ingredients) one may seem unprincipled or indefinite and fail to develop any special strengths to cope *practically* with new situations.

The conformity problem can pose itself in irritating ways where people in authority (heads, teachers, tutors) seem to be obsessed by some limited aspect of educational policy or technique. One wants better discipline, another more exciting work. One is a stickler for neat blackboards, another goes apoplectic over divergencies of dress or hair style. One sells the cult of personal relationship, another wonders which union you intend to join. One expects attendance at school worship as a matter of expediency if not principle, another wonders whether young people have any principles at all these days.

The occasional irritation arising from extreme conformism can be well-matched by non-conforming extremists, who equally seem to think that only their personal views and styles are of any consequence. One can only suggest that the path of mutual irritation seems profitless, and that it is practical to search for as much common ground as possible rather than make an excessive display of idiosyncratic principle. Superficial features like appearance, manners, and style are not purely personal, for they typically declare particular attitudes to the world and other people, but neither are they the central problems of education. They are important tokens but need not be identified completely with underlying realities, for a bold front may express either underlying boldness or underlying apprehensiveness.

One can be fully personal, fully oneself, only with people known intimately and trustingly. Even a mature professional person gives only part of himself in his work. Those who aspire to total work-dedication are not necessarily better either at their work or to live with. It would seem unrealistic, therefore, to suggest that a student teacher can be even his full professional self as he enters a situation which is hardly known at all and where trust has yet to be established on all sides. Nevertheless, this cautious line of thought does point to a practical way forward. The beginner can think in terms of trying to be himself (and not some false front) as he enters the teaching practice situation. And he can think in terms of encouraging trust, for example, by seeking help from those able to give it, by giving help in small matters until skill is developed in helping with large matters, and by extra attention to the many small courtesies that help people feel that their interest and effort are worth giving.

It must be obvious that the tenor of this argument favours subtlety and sophistication in thought and action, and not simplistic slogans. If one had, nevertheless, to list a few maxims to guide initial practical action, they might be:

1 Search for common ground as a basis for co-operation rather than flaunt divergency.

2 In complementation of the first maxim, try in due course to bring your personal viewpoints and skills to bear in those parts of the school work where they can be exploited most constructively.

3 Concentrate immediately on what you can rather than on what you cannot do, and on smaller tasks until you gradually move on to larger.

4 Build up a picture of the school and its tasks by observation and regular consultation with those prepared to advise. Some of the systematic points for consideration were mentioned in the first chapter—(a) school size and organization, (b) buildings and equipment, (c) social background, (d) educational aims and attitudes, (e) staffing, (f) range of pupils and especially the character of classes and pupils one may be teaching, (g) curricula and syllabuses, (h) methods and resources, (i) the character of the general social life and discipline, (j) attitudes and practices in relation to training young teachers.

5 Avoid facile conclusions; be patient with the complexities of education; if one thing fails try another; respect and consult the regular teachers whose work you are being allowed to interrupt.

These maxims may seem rather obvious, but they remain relevant to the common difficulties of beginning teachers in (a) formulating appropriate (and appropriately modest) aims, (b) in assessing the capacities of younger and often slower learners, (c) in making full use of the professional advice on the spot (which is ironically sometimes withheld unless asked, because teachers laudably do not want to seem interfering), and (d) in coming to see how the whole character of a school and its environment bears on each individual lesson, as much as the character of what is taught or the specific method of teaching.

First impressions

Before making any further suggestions, it may be useful to consider some aspects of teaching practice as it strikes student teachers directly. For example, Edith Cope (1971), in a study of the school experience of students in two colleges of education, reminds one afresh of the diversity of circumstances already stressed in the preceding chapter. Ten per cent of the sample of students were teaching classes of more than forty pupils, while another 10 per cent had classes of less than twenty. One quarter of the classes were streamed (that is, constituted according to apparent general ability) while the other three-quarters were mixed-ability classes. One quarter of the students were not able to use a school staffroom—commonly because there was none.

About three-quarters found the class or subject teacher helpful or very helpful, but almost one in ten found him difficult or somewhat difficult. About one half found supervisors constructive and encouraging, but 40 per cent saw supervisors in a neutral light and 12 per cent saw them as rather discouraging and unconstructive.

Students found teaching practice rewarding mainly because of the opportunity of working with children, being a working member of a school community, and having the chance of trying out ideas and theories in a practical situation (in that order of merit). They found the practice frustrating mainly because of its limited length, the necessity of accepting the presence and authority of others in the classroom, and because of the supervisory and assessment procedures (again in that order of importance). One of the first practical needs that Cope's students seemed to feel was for a human response from the children. There seems to have been apprehension that one might simply not get through to the children at all. Observation alone was not as satisfying as interacting with the pupils, however simply.

Student, teacher, and tutor perceived the teaching practice situation in different ways. Students and teachers tended to think that assessment was considered important, whereas supervisors thought of themselves as guides rather than assessors. Teachers thought of themselves as being sympathetic and welcoming to the students more than the students thought of the teachers as being sympathetic and welcoming. Over half of the teachers were uncertain about what the college expected of them. This phenomenon can be matched among some secondary teachers responsible for graduate students. The present author has met several experienced teachers who were glad to be reassured that one trusted them to use their own professional discretion in providing whatever pattern of teaching experience seemed best in the circumstances.

While the Cope enquiry highlights some features of school practice that may be quite general, it is necessary to remember that it was an enquiry at one place and time. Things must be expected to differ at other places and times, whether slightly or radically. Furthermore, it would be unrealistic to imagine that all of the imperfections in a human situation can be eliminated. People with different roles are bound frequently to see the same situation in different terms. It could not be otherwise. And the fact that one feature or another is found satisfying or frustrating is not by itself sufficient to make that feature commendable or damnable without qualification. For example, the fact that the process of assessment is not in itself enjoyable does not mean that assessment can be avoided. Nor can one be deceived by any suggestion that assessment is entirely dispensable, or, alternatively, can be done in some unspecified painless way. People will assess one another in some fashion or other, and any assessment may bring pain to a proportion of them. Teaching and learning are almost bound to be accompanied by some frustration, and yet the path of temporary frustration can lead to some of the greatest eventual successes.

Just as the partly frustrating may be necessary or desirable for some further end, so what is satisfying may be gratuitously so without serving any further worthwhile purpose. For example, working with children could be a self-indulging pastime (albeit a masochistic one on occasions) that fails to further the children's education in any distinctive way; or enjoying membership of a working school community might happen to mean enjoying educational aims and methods that are open to grave challenge. It would be perverse and discouraging to suggest that one should seek out frustration and eschew the path of satisfaction, but the limitations of the opposite policy also need recognition.

Some graduate student teachers were invited to mention what problems of teaching practice seemed important to them after their first short practice of three weeks, mainly in primary schools. They put their fingers shrewdly on some important points. It was difficult to know what to expect of children, and surprising how simple one had to try and be:

> One of the main difficulties encountered is getting down to the level of the children's understanding and gauging their capacity to absorb new facts. You have to remember that while at primary school they are still completely children with no adult conceptions or judgments. This means that all subjects have to be pruned down and simplified into easily comprehensible terms.

And another commented:

> I was very disappointed with some of the written work I received as a result of my early lessons. To some extent I could improve it by modifying my approach, but, after consultation with other members of the staff, I also realised that my standards were too high for the children concerned.

Of course, it pays to expect high standards, provided that the pupils have at least a chance of getting near to them.

There was insight into some of the precise but varied significance of the teacher's role.

> The teacher is there to help and lead towards adulthood, as well as 'teach' the child knowledge which one hopes is remembered and understood.

To observe teachers actually doing the job is very important. Contact with these teachers is valuable. They know the children concerned and can give one down to earth advice on handling the class.

The wide diversity of skills expected of junior school teachers also surprised me—not only proficiency in mathematics and english, history, and geography, but also in such subjects as dance, singing, drama, and sewing.

With this insight went uncertainty about the student's own capacity or best line of attack:

Should we concentrate on approach and control of the class, or content of the lesson, or trying out as many and varied visual aids as possible, or getting through a set amount of work, or. . . . ?

Not all lessons can be expected to be spectacular and abundant in the use of visual aids. A lot of groundwork is covered in lessons which are mundane and ordinary.

I found it difficult to think of things for the children to do for fifty minutes in *every* lesson.

This last remark can be matched by the comment of a young graduate history teacher after her first month of regular teaching service (she had just got her first salary), that the non-stop character of her teaching responsibilities left her rather breathless.

Another young graduate, towards the end of his initial professional course, stimulated by Hannam, Smyth and Stephenson's *Young Teachers and Reluctant Learners* (1971), discussed school practice in more radical and sceptical terms:

The way the school practice game is set up, theory is forgotten and the aim is to become a competent practitioner, not a high-flying transformer or a speechless sack of nerves. . . . The student sees himself as an anomic being trying to win the approval of headmaster, supervisor, children, and teachers. . . . The head may mention things about his staff and the staff about the head to the student. The student may feel that he is being used as a free period tool for the teacher and the teacher may even see the student as a disrupter and intruder. . . . The school is hierarchical, authoritarian, paternalistic, and insulated from the world at large in some ways. Learning is at present identified with a competitive scrambling for marks, the fruits of office are a reward for social conformity.

This challenge to the system is rather facile, giving inadequate recognition to the inevitability of at least some of these generalities in any educational system, however radicalized.

None the less, there is certainly a discussable point of view here, with possible practical implications for even the beginning teacher:

> Young teachers are often committed to liberal and progressive educational ideals. Yet they find it hard to believe that everyone is not motivated by the same carrots that were held out to them.

It may be another practical maxim to identify the positive values in the social backgrounds of pupils who are not predestined for middle class scholasticism. But, if there is a need to counter-balance the exclusiveness of allegedly middle-class ideals, there remains the problem of giving all children access to the human heritage, regardless of class. To pursue the problem of the relationship between social class loyalties and educational entitlements would rapidly lead far from the immediate practical problems of beginning teachers.

Teaching skills

What are the first skills that teachers require? The young graduate in a primary school was struck by the number and variety of skills that seemed necessary. As a wider range of pupils have come to receive a longer period of secondary education teachers have increasingly recognized the need there too for quite wide-ranging skills. Even in universities there is greater concern with problems of teaching, counselling, and human relationships generally, in addition to those of scholarship and research.

The fact that there has been a growing demand for the individual teacher with a wider range of skills obviously does not mean that everyone can be omnicompetent. There must be division of teaching labour. Furthermore, there will normally be some teaching skills which have a stronger market position than others, so that a person with a relatively rare specialist skill will be welcome even without a wide range of other skills. The skill might be in the intellectual grooming of sixth-form mathematics specialists, the development of high musical standards throughout a school, the organization of first-rate opportunities in games and physical education, or the devising and implementation of special reading programmes for slow learners. Skills like these, although specialist in one sense, are sufficiently wide-ranging to require no extra justification.

Some teaching skills that suggest themselves immediately as being important are the following:

1 Skill in formulating clearly to oneself and others what objective is to be achieved by the teaching and learning.

2 Skill in influencing and controlling other people's behaviour—in communication or interpersonal relationship as it is sometimes rather vaguely called.

3 Skill in specific subjects—mathematics, literature, cooking, reading, musical performance, painting, history, etc.

4 Skill in observing and assessing what is happening, in the sense of recognizing the significance of what can be observed, and of assessing what has been achieved after any unit of teaching.

5 Skill in organizing physical situations, material resources, and the co-operation of other people, in aid of any teaching enterprise.

These skills overlap with one another. Skill in understanding clearly what cooking or mathematics is about contributes to skill in formulating teaching objectives, and in assessing how far the objectives are attained. It also helps the skill of human control, in so far as one at least knows what one is trying to do. Learners are not willing to be controlled by someone who does not understand even his own specialism. Beginning teachers commonly cannot avoid having to try and teach some things which they do not fully understand themselves, but it is a good idea to contrive as much practice as possible in teaching things that are grasped fully in one's own mind. Even with new and unfamiliar material that may have been prepared only the previous night, it is worth trying to concentrate on what one can fully understand, rather than resorting to echoing from text-books and reference books a mass of unrelated detail which is no more likely to convince the pupil than the teacher himself.

Overlapping is also illustrated in the skills of controlling people and organizing material resources. A teacher who has or cultivates a friendly but self-assured manner with pupils is better able to get their co-operation in using material resources in an orderly manner. There will be less mess, less waste, less disorder. But, similarly, the teacher who plans the use of resources systematically can control the pupils better. He checks in advance that the right quantities of necessary books or materials will be available, that apparatus is working and can be operated in the particular room available. He has contingency plans for broken pencil points (have spares), forgotten or misplaced books (share with your neighbour), finished jotters (have spares or know where to send for them), things dropped, broken, or spilled (get one person to clear up; insist on the rest getting on with their own work). He gradually gets the pupils trained in dealing automatically by approved methods with a whole range of typical eventualities, so that none of these distracts from the ongoing learning programme.

As a final example in the meantime, skill in observing and assessing what pupils are doing is a necessary partner of skill in control and of skill in redefining objectives from time to time. A beginner may be apprehensive about what will be seen if one really looks. Consequently, mischief may quietly or noisily grow while the teacher's gaze is fixed on his lesson notes. To take a good regular look at each part of the class is worth more than constant checking that the lesson plan is being strictly followed. Alternatively, the young teacher sees perfectly well that trouble is brewing in the far corner, but hopes that it will subside; or he confuses authority with authoritarianism and fails to intervene. Too much intervention can admittedly create its own problems, but an early admonition in a friendly manner may help teacher and taught where even a vigorous reproof may fail if it is belated.

Observing what the pupils are doing is not, of course, mainly a question of looking for the worst in the form of incipient misconduct. It is even more important to observe whether they really understand instructions and explanations, and whether they have the intellectual and physical means to complete any exercise or activity to which they are directed. Accustoming oneself to observe the progress of class activities (taking care not to become exclusively preoccupied for long with any one individual or group) helps to bring out cases where the objective has proved too demanding or insufficiently demanding. The objective then has to be redefined or extra means of achieving it have to be supplied.

The five skills listed above are interdependent. And, to be more precise, they are five categories of skill rather than five skills. Any one category invites extensive subdivision into a large number of skills that are nearer to being unitary in character, although even relatively simple unitary skills tend to be further subdivisible if it is desired to pursue them in detail. Skill in using a blackboard is a kind of unitary pedagogic skill, but it could be divided into different sub-skills, such as setting out a mathematical argument as clearly and concisely as possible, drawing good geographical outlines, using neat and legible lettering, planning the use of blackboard space where it is intended to build up any pattern bit by bit, or even the tiny sub-skill of holding the chalk (not like a pencil) so that it does not crack in two pieces to the merriment of pupils and the detriment of discipline.

Skill 1 in formulating immediate objectives depends on knowing the current programme, the capacities of the pupils, the available resources, one's own strengths and weaknesses in the area involved, the time available, and the physical circumstances. It is skill in identifying the strong and weak potential of a complex situation; and, for the beginner, in identifying where the objective of improving one's own teaching skill can really connect with the objectives which the pupils and the regular teacher feel themselves to have. To begin with, it is very much skill in accurate observing of the facts of a given situation, which may not accord with expectation and may upset ideal or long-term objectives. It is a skill, therefore, in adaptation to circumstances in the short-run without surrendering larger objectives in the long run, in realism without cynicism, in pursuing modest but achievable aims. It depends on sheer experience, but also on studying the psychology of children at particular stages of development, and the resources and techniques available to pursue whatever goals are recognized for each stage. It is not so much a question of spanning some imagined gap between practice and theory at the point of widest separation, but more of moving an actual situation a small way in the direction of what would be better.

Skill 2 in influencing and controlling other people's behaviour is one in which there is very wide differentiation before anyone even starts to teach. To be realistic, one must neither underestimate the persisting advantage or disadvantage of the teacher's social skills or personality built up over the vital first two decades of life, nor, on the other hand, the extent to which people can develop and change, particularly if they are brought into circumstances which exert different and persistent pressures. The fact that there is no one exclusive way of effective human control means that teachers with quite different qualities achieve control in their own way. Some are naturally self-assured, others deliberately brash; some rather noisy, others very quiet; some given to irony, others to humour; some distantly cool, others intimately warm; some respected for extra-curricular enthusiasm, others for general organizing flair.

Apart from such differences in style, there is a wide difference in the kinds of situation that have to be controlled. One need only think of the differing approaches suitable for, let us say, a first infants class, a class of eleven-year-olds, a group of less academic school leavers, a sixth form preparing for college or university entry, a class of student teachers, a science laboratory class, a physical education class, a girls' independent school class, a remedial reading class, etc. There may be broad principles of control that run through diverse teaching situations—showing respect and consideration for people, making one's expectations clear, commending what is well done and reproving what is bad, relating work tasks to the learner's existing capacities and interests, accepting and expressing the genuine right to authority given to a teacher by his office—but, in detailed practical terms, these principles imply quite different action in the different circumstances illustrated. The detail is so important that the excellent science master might be a flop in the remedial class, the professor in the first infants, the infant mistress in the lecture room, the independent school mistress in the urban slum school, or the secondary comprehensive housemaster among a set of sixth-form high flyers.

Skill 3 in specific subjects is part of the skill of teaching these subjects. Absence of subject skill contributes fairly conspicuously to teaching defects, even although its presence is not alone sufficient for teaching success. Defects in teaching method are more likely to be seen as teaching defects, but defects in knowledge or understanding of subjects can also contribute. There is perhaps some reluctance to think of the subject specialist as defective in his subject. It detracts rather seriously from common and convenient assumptions. But there are various ways in which this can happen.

A graduate may obtain an admirable degree in, let us say, history or literature and yet have had no time to grow familiar with large tracts between the topics he happened to specialize in, although these may be tracts that are expected to be cultivated in school syllabuses. Second, any student may have made himself proficient (and many do) in the skill of transmuting the study of his subject into essays and examination answers but have little skill in transmuting it into other possible things—for example, enlightened conversation, the relation of his discipline to similar or different disciplines or to life in general, or into lessons for different groups of pupils. The graduate with a good honours degree may fall back desperately on the nourishment of some school text-book to prepare his lesson.

Third, the highly trained student may have no personal commitment to his subject, except as a means to a livelihood. This sometimes shows itself in a lack of keen interest in what he has just studied intensively for three years. Perhaps the excesses of academicism generate a degree of revolt, so that graduation is at once followed by a distaste for intellectual enquiry, and the activity of serious reading dies rapidly away, if it was established in the first instance. The inevitably large gap between what graduates can do and what children can do may encourage the flight from college or university values, although many of the intellectual values of higher education are equally relevant, in an appropriate form, for earlier stages of education, and teaching is impoverished where they are absent.

Skill 4 in observing and assessing learners is so complex that one would have to study large areas of educational psychology to understand it fully. The student teacher faces an extra problem in addition to his inexperience, his limited study of psychology, and the ordinary hazards of bias and selectivity that enter into all observing. The problem is that what may help the beginner to understand and analyse his teaching experience may readily give offence to the regular practitioners who make the experience possible in the first instance.

To keep a critical record of one's experience is an obvious means of self-training in observation and analysis. But, because beginners are beginners, they are liable in all naïvety to write or say things that are taken amiss. Even where a student is neither naïve nor given to tactlessness in general, a reference to an 'old-fashioned' text-book or even a mention that a school does x but not y may be seen as presumptuous or hostile. To keep any kind of record is to distance oneself in part from the ongoing action, to be less than 'one of us'— adding insult to injury, since, as a student, one is not fully one of them any way.

The inevitable outcome of this is that frank discussion of what is observed may have to be reserved for informal occasions among friends who enjoy mutual confidence. It can hardly be otherwise, for few bodies of people can be expected to welcome the appraisal of someone who is both a beginner and an outsider. Observe but keep one's counsel seems the only practical policy. The necessity of this underlines the notion of teaching as an initiation into the ways of particular teaching institutions, rather than a specific training in agreed objectives and techniques, against which the institutions themselves should be measured.

These limitations are not perhaps so serious in practice as in contemplation. There are many regular teachers who are perfectly open-minded about teaching practices and do not disdain the views or endeavours even of beginners. There are national discussions of objectives and methods which give public currency to criticisms which schools have to notice and may even act on. There are areas where teachers have co-operated in quite searchingly analytic studies of their own teaching activities. The publicity now given to positive initiatives in education and to outstanding examples of good practice encourages more positive rather than negative thinking generally. But it remains that practical policy for the beginner must be to reserve his more critical observations for his own meditation or for discussion with those in whom he can really confide.

Skill 5 in organizing means mainly lesson preparation and class management for the beginner. Some practical points have already been made, and others will be more fully discussed in the next chapters. A Scottish teacher (Stewart, 1972) included the following in his golden rules for beginners—(1) Be there first, (2) Be prepared, and (3) Keep them busy, but yourself free. Another common exhortation is to think of yourself as a manager of learning activities and not just as a teacher. The point of this is illustrated in the common beginning practice of talking too much and not getting the pupils to answer enough questions or do enough practical work. The beginner is understandably concerned with his own performance although it is the learners' performance that matters. But he can console himself with the fact that mature teachers have not always learned this lesson.

An aspect of organization that proves difficult for many beginners arises from the fact that more classes now are divided into small groups doing different things. It is no easy matter to keep this kind of learning situation going effectively. Beginners should really get the chance to work with perhaps one group alone in the first instance, and only gradually broaden out towards the more complex problem. It is a bad induction to small-group teaching to have to cope with its total complexity right at the start. This is a problem that regular teachers and supervisors should prevent.

Over the threshold

This sub-heading is a good summing up of the position of most beginning teachers after quite a short period of teaching practice. Some feel hesitant for a longer period. Some feel hardly any hesitancy at all. Some are over the threshold of that practice, although not necessarily over the threshold of longer-term commitment to teaching. Some are bound to be in schools where teaching is more difficult even for the experienced. But most find rapidly that they can make contact with pupils and teachers, that there is help available if only they can bring themselves to use it, that one can survive and sometimes flourish, that one may even gradually make a genuine small contribution to the learning and life of the school and be appreciated for it by the regular teachers.

The problem of student-teacher status is inescapable. The best attitude for both the student and the regular staff is to avoid either concealing or emphasizing the beginner's status. One wants to accept it but get on with the practical job and the steady march towards full professional responsibility. Wherever one stands on the conformism-radicalism spectrum, the beginner can acquire and improve his basic teaching skills only by a considerable degree of conformity with those who let him share their work, and who, in some cases, will be more radical than him anyway. The general question of conformity and radicalism in education will always be open for debate.

This chapter has drawn a rough map of teaching skills, identified special problems that face the beginner, and made several practical recommendations which will be more fully developed in the next chapters. It might conclude with two general suggestions. The first is for that majority of situations in which most beginners are succeeding either moderately or very well. The suggestion is that professionalism consists partly in continuing to strive for further improvement even if what is already done is tolerable.

The second is for that minority of situations in which one finds that things are going all wrong. The suggestion here is that, just as one swallow does not make a summer, one icicle does not make a winter. Ask advice from anyone likely to help, talk about your feelings to your close friends, consider what circumstances were disadvantageous to your efforts, try something different next time.

Questions
of discipline

3

It is a common assumption that young teachers are particularly concerned about problems of discipline and a common criticism of professional courses that such problems receive insufficient practical attention. It is because of this assumption that one hastens to give the topic prompt attention in the present context. However, there is a deeper paradox behind this apparently straightforward situation. There are very many beginners who are not really faced by any serious disciplinary problems, either because the objective conditions of indiscipline do not prevail or because the beginner soon develops skill in coping with any indiscipline that does arise. Such teachers may, in a sense, not be profoundly interested in questions of discipline.

The other aspect of the paradox is that beginners who have more serious disciplinary problems are liable to want urgent recipes for their specific problems. They want to know how to pick today's chestnuts out of the fire, not next week's or next year's. To take a different metaphor, they want to know how to treat the symptoms more urgently than they want to know how to analyse the causes. They too, in a sense, may not be profoundly interested in questions of discipline but only in first-aid for emergencies. Concern about immediate palliatives is perfectly natural and legitimate, but, even to be practical, long-term as well as short-term perspectives are valuable. Many short-term crises—particularly when one follows another persistently—arise from failure to identify underlying problems that need radical solutions. Some of these radical solutions may be within the teacher's or school's power, even if everyone recognizes that others depend on things beyond the control of a teacher or school.

Various meanings; various kinds of problem

Another source of confusion is the fact that people pretending to talk about the problem of discipline commonly obscure the existence of quite different kinds of disciplinary problems and quite different meanings of the term 'discipline'. For some an enquiry about discipline signifies an enquiry into whether pupils are caned, strapped, paddled, slippered, ear-pulled, knuckle-rapped, tongue-lashed, put 'on report', sent to the Head, reported to parents, detained after school, set punishment exercises, deprived of privileges, or referred to psychologist or counsellor. It is an enquiry about official and unofficial 'deterrents', about local custom and the likely source of effective results. For others discipline apparently can only mean self-discipline and anything else is to be called external control or the maintenance of order. For others again discipline means mainly the distinctive influence exercised by various studies and activities because of their intrinsic nature. Rightly or wrongly, team games have been thought to foster co-operative discipline, physical exercise to distract from impure thought, Latin or mathematics to sharpen reasoning power, craft work to compel respect for the objective possibilities of materials, philosophy to encourage rationality and detachment.

In addition to differences of meaning of the kind just suggested, there is a distinction between the philosophical problem of *justifying* the alleged aim of any disciplinary procedure or attitude and the technical problem of showing that one procedure rather than another is the better practical way of achieving the aim. For example, critics of corporal punishment may argue both against the justifiability of corporal punishment and against its technical efficiency in achieving its supposed aim. If the latter aim were to deter from repetition of a misdemeanour, they might argue that misdemeanours are often continued after punishment, just as recidivists repeat the crimes for which they have already been imprisoned.

Arguments about discipline characteristically drift almost imperceptibly between these different kinds of question, to which different kinds of evidence are relevant. Moreover, even if one clearly distinguishes the two kinds of problem, each kind of evidence is in itself difficult to evaluate. People have different notions of human value, of what are legitimate ways of regarding one another. They also have different experiences and understandings of what actual procedures produce what definite effects. This means that the problem has to be pursued in two areas where probabilities, not certainties, must suffice. Recognition of this inevitable fact is another first step towards being practical about discipline, that is, towards pursuing what is practicable and justifiable.

Distinguishing the practicable and the justifiable does not mean detaching them completely from one another. Some disciplinary actions misfire because they are felt strongly to be unwarranted. It is a question of principle that makes them also technically ineffective. The worm turns. The discipline is flatly rejected. Of course, where no one disputes the disciplinary judgement in relation to an agreed aim, the aim itself might become tarnished by association with a misconceived disciplinary technique (perhaps punishing all for the fault of one? withdrawing a privilege which turns out to be higher in the hierarchy of importance than one had appreciated? mistaking who among several was the real culprit in some affray?). The interrelation of justifiability and practicability is well illustrated in that universal question about how quiet or noisy a class of children should be. To give two examples: tutor A comments, 'I don't know how you managed to work among so much noise; it would have driven me crazy' (Student-teacher: 'That was my best class'). Tutor B comments to another student, 'Do you always have them so quiet? Don't you think there could be a bit more activity and talk without disturbing anybody?' (Head: 'She has very good class control—keeps them working away nice and quietly').

The argument so far has been that one should distinguish but also interrelate disciplinary aims and techniques, and that part of the meaning of being practical about discipline consists in recognizing that one is dealing inescapably with probabilities, sometimes only possibilities, rather than certainty. Part of the problem of discipline is this problem of tolerating some degree of uncertainty. Beyond these general features that run through all disciplinary questions, it is detailed appraisal of the precise character of different educational situations that is most important for the development of effective discipline. Where discipline is felt to be a problem of any seriousness it is also necessary to think in terms of diverse remedies and partial successes, not, as the beginner may understandably hope, in terms of simple remedies and dramatic success.

Immediately practical considerations

Before looking more deeply into factors underlying discipline it may be worth outlining some considerations that offer a basis for immediate planning and action by a beginning teacher. They represent a check list against which to assess intentions, achievements, and required modifications. The first item is a reminder of the main sources of discipline or indiscipline—teachers themselves, the pupils, the school, and society outside the school. Teachers vary in temperamental traits, intelligence, interest in children and what they are supposed to teach, and in mastery of professional skills, such as skill in communicating clearly, strongly, and sympathetically. Pupils vary in personality, intelligence, motivation, exposure to diverse and powerful social backgrounds, and degree of emotional normality or disturbance. Schools vary in tradition, aim, atmosphere, curriculum, organization, methods, and staffing. Social areas vary in tradition, prosperity, homogeneity, stability, law-abidingness, occupational patterns, and enthusiasm towards the idea of education.

Schools and societies cannot usually be changed quickly and dramatically and, therefore, it seems more immediately practical to think about teachers and pupils. Teachers are paid to produce, or at least facilitate, certain kinds of change. Pupils have the pliability of youth, even if there are problems about the direction in which the pliability operates. Although teachers can, in principle, exert most influence by temporary or relatively permanent changes in their own behaviour, it has to be recognized that inevitable proximity to one's own behaviour by no means ensures understanding of that behaviour or facility in altering its patterns. This means, paradoxically, that the point where practical action seems most feasible may, in the worst cases, be almost as immune to desirable change as some tough structural feature of society itself. A good example is the resistance of established speech patterns to radical change, which makes advice to 'cultivate a well modulated voice' rather empty if such a voice does not already exist. However, it is obvious that some behavioural patterns can be changed if the person wants to change them, develops some understanding of how to change them, and is more highly rewarded for the new pattern. This is sometimes exemplified by a young teacher performing in a rather mediocre way as a student but much better once he is employed as a teacher in a situation where he is financially rewarded for a clearly specified performance.

Self-understanding is not simply an intellectual indulgence, a private benefit. It is a vital element in the practical problem of identifying strengths and weaknesses, more and less modifiable patterns, in relation to the requirements and problems of the teaching task. Some examples may serve to illustrate the general point. A considerable number of teachers lack a sense of definite or enthusiastic commitment to the profession for which they are preparing or which they have entered. This conflicts with the image of the born or dedicated teacher, and yet many of these unsurely committed teachers soon find themselves making a thoroughly professional contribution to education, for teaching requires cool and patient professionalism as much as passionate dedication. It is practical to recognize and accept the particular balance of the two attitudes that happens to characterize one's own outlook.

As a second example, one might contrast the socially and verbally facile teacher with the teacher who is more inhibited and anxious. Either of these might teach excellently according to his own style, but one could imagine extreme cases where the first rested on his social skills, conducted classes fluently and happily, but failed to put any intellectual substance or structure into a lesson, while the second had so fully prepared and structured the intellectual substance that he neglected the social channels through which the substance must go if it is to enter into the pupil's reality. Although the contrast is exaggerated, this is one of the major balancing problems confronting young teachers.

These examples based on attitude and personality can be completed with a final example based on education and training. Most teachers specialize to some extent even if only in terms of their own personal interests. Many are quite highly specialized—teaching only art or mathematics or whatever it may be. This specialization of interest or skill is obviously both necessary and desirable. It gives children a wider variety of stimulation and a wider choice from which to develop their own interests and skills. At the same time the strengths and advantages of this specialization are accompanied by a danger of being blinkered within the horizons of the specialism. This is most dramatically exemplified in the case of graduate specialists, who, after three or four years' exposure to specialist training, are sometimes almost like infants again if confronted by the challenge of a subject different from their own. Scientists may be alarmed by the thought of writing a short essay ('I haven't done anything like that for five or six years') or literary specialists by the simplest exercises in statistics. Self-understanding, therefore, is not just a question of plumbing the subconscious depths of personality, but also of recognizing the true character and limitations of the particular education one has had out of the many that were theoretically possible. It is only reasonable for the specialist to offer his specialism in the strongest way possible, but he may fall short even in doing that if he forgets that there are other specialisms and, more important, other things than specialism.

Although self-understanding is immediately, permanently, and vitally related to successful discipline, it is obviously not something that can be achieved quickly by applying any simple technique. There is even a danger that understanding becomes an excuse for inaction, for fatalistic acceptance. The second practical maxim now to be suggested is a corrective. It is that the teacher's duty is to control a certain kind of situation and that acceptance of the responsibility for control is a prime requirement for successful discipline, that is, for achieving whatever the educational objective is with the maximum economy and minimum disturbance. Problems are few where the teacher is temperamentally ready to exercise control or where there is little resistance to control in any case. The problem increases as these conditions cease to be satisfied. It is then that the young teacher thinks—Should I have been less friendly and complaisant to begin with? How firm can I be when the regular teacher is the person really in charge of the class? Will it damage my assessment for class control if I call in assistance or send a pupil to the Head? Can you really blame the pupils for their bad behaviour in view of their disadvantageous social background? Why should middle-class standards of conduct be expected anyway? Am I expecting too much/too little from the class? Is it not better for the children to be free rather than constrained? Will they not learn more if they are encouraged rather than discouraged?

Questions like these may be partly the cause of young teachers' uncertainties about discipline, or they may be rationalizations of failure to achieve sufficient control. There is plenty of scope for debate about the objectives of educational control, but there is no escaping the fact that teachers are necessary only if they try to shape children in ways that the community feels is worth its money. Nor is it any cogent argument to suggest that controlling or shaping other people is an abuse of individual freedom and autonomy. Mutual control and influence are inescapable in any case. The most consistent prophets of non-interference interfere at least tacitly by their existence and example with more activist philosophies of life, and, one suspects, often intend to. Even where genuine non-interference is greatest, this represents a decisive exposure of young people to the forces of ignorance or chance. Control is not abused by being exercised, since its exercise is inevitable, but by being exercised in an offensive manner or towards ends which themselves are unjustifiable.

The young teacher has to struggle both with the problem of working out his own aims, although these cannot have been either fully thought out or extensively tested against actual educational conditions, and with the problem of developing specific disciplinary skills. The immediate practical remedy may be to work at those aims and techniques which are already embodied in the educational situation and which are most congenial, or least uncongenial, to his own feelings about education. There is plenty of time to work outwards towards aims and techniques that may be different, perhaps eventually radically different, from what prevails at present. Instant radicalism may have the greater rhetorical appeal, but gradualism is the path of practicality.

Confused thinking about freedom and about social class helps to sustain some young teachers' disciplinary problems. On the freedom question an important point is that there are many different freedoms and constraints. Certain freedoms exclude others. All freedoms operate amid unavoidable constraints (the paradox of freedom).

There are times and places when children should be free to be noisy, despite the resulting constraint on the peace of the neighbouring adults. There are other occasions when children should be freed from the constraints of their own noisiness so that they and others can benefit from activities which require a modicum of quiet and order. What teachers need to develop is not a passion for freedom or constraint, but a just sense of occasion. On the social class question there is a danger of making glib assumptions about the definition and characteristics of social classes despite the controversial nature of this problem. It seems more important to consider what children have a right to as human beings, including initiation into the general idea of moral behaviour (as distinct from highly specific moral creeds), rather than to agonize about their social class membership.

Also, it does not follow from the fact that one can trace causal patterns in human behaviour that these patterns exercise some inescapable and overriding force. Social and psychological patterns are certainly forces to be reckoned with, but so is the force of rationality—not, obviously, as a guaranteed way of changing behaviour, but as a challenge to partial views, a challenge which can be escaped only if one contracts out of *all* self-justification and not just out of the area of justification that happens to be inconvenient at a particular time. A certain social background may make certain educational aims more difficult to achieve, but it is obvious from social history that people do overcome social handicaps, and it detracts from the dignity of the individual to treat him as if he were socially imprisoned. Treating children as if they cannot be expected to accept responsibility itself encourages irresponsibility. An over-simplified view of social or psychological determinism should not stand between a young teacher and effective class control.

What then is to be done once these possible misconceptions have been set aside? Morrison and McIntyre (1969) make three good points about class control. The first is that the teacher must watch the class and make them feel that he knows what is going on. This is helped if the teacher trains himself to think in terms of a programme of work for the class rather than a programme of exposition by the teacher. This does not mean excluding exposition but only subordinating it. Positive attention to the class is also helped by taking care to leave time for questions, answers, discussion, clarification, revision, and digression, and by commenting regularly and definitely on the behaviour and work of the class and its members as this seems appropriate. This is not meant to conjure up a vision of the nagging teacher, but rather to dispel a vision of the teacher who usurps all of the time with his exposition, fails to give the pupils much to do, and says little about their achievements and shortcomings.

The second point is that all transitional points are potential foci of trouble—the arrival and departure of the class, a change during the lesson to a different kind of work, the interruption by some class visitor. Pupils have to be trained in appropriate ways of behaving in transitional situations and have to be allowed sufficient time to make any necessary change. Everyone knows how irritating it is to be called away from a task that is just moving to its conclusion, and yet pupils are often expected to make remarkably quick shifts among radically different activities. It helps to keep pupils informed about the pattern of their work, to warn them of the imminent end of the time allowed for any section of it, to reassure them if they fail to finish or are interrupted by some special happening, and to avoid excessive chopping and changing of routines. The young teacher sometimes plans his lesson to the last minute, but it is useful to consider what you would do if you do not get started properly in the first five minutes, or if you are not finished when the bell rings, or if you finish five minutes before the end of a period. There are some obvious possibilities. Have some small section of your lesson that can be either included or excluded, depending on how the time goes. Have some extension of the lesson or a selection of time-fillers for the lesson that ends too soon (revision questions round the class, brief discussion of a quite different topic of current interest, tell the class about what they will be doing in the forthcoming lessons).

The third point has already been suggested. It is the danger of prematurely adopting a too permissive attitude towards the class. Apart from the ideological mistakes already mentioned, over-permissiveness sometimes arises from an excessive, although laudable, desire to be nice to the children or to win their esteem. For anyone seriously afflicted by this tendency, John Ezard's comment (Kemble, 1971) is perhaps not too frank—'You may make them love you one day but the next day they will shit on you.' Since student teachers are by definition students as well as teachers, they sometimes bring to the world of schools and children the casual fraternal attitudes that are appropriate to colleges and universities. It is to be hoped that this is not an entirely bad thing, but it can be treacherous. Even adolescent pupils, and still more junior school children, are not college students and they are not comrades in any sense of being on a really equal footing. They can and should be treated in a friendly manner, but the teacher-pupil relationship is bound to be friendliness with a difference. Evans (1965) makes the point that 'permissiveness conveys the idea that no value is attached to any particular attitudes, and it also fails to ensure that children practise the behaviour which results from holding particular attitudes.' Gammage (1971) in realistic tone suggests that 'at secondary school level a mixture of both tradition and concrete survival tactics usually demands that the teacher "defines" the situation before the pupils do'—the last point reminding one of the special importance of first encounters.

After self-understanding and acceptance of the responsibility for exercising control a set of three bipolar factors are important for practical disciplinary control. They are (a) preparedness combined with adaptability, (b) concern for the pupils as persons combined with concern for the educative tasks that will develop their best potentialities, and (c) attention to motivation combined with attention to achievement. Preparedness is, of course, a counsel of perfection, for it is the unexpected that so often puts things wrong. Similarly, adaptation sounds all very well, but circumstances have a habit of overwhelming our powers of adaptation. Nonetheless, there are practical strategies (or stratagems?) that can be helpful. Suggestions have just been offered about the timing and mistiming of lessons. It might be useful (i) to keep a list of unexpected disciplinary situations, the way they were handled in fact, and the way you would handle them another time in the light of reflection; (ii) to think about the typical characteristics of pupils of the ages you will be required to deal with, about the kinds of rewards and kinds of admonition you might use; (iii) to list things that should be avoided as being most likely to create offence or touch off unnecessarily abrasive confrontations.

Beginners are understandably concerned with their own preparation and achievement. This needs to be modified gradually towards a greater concern with arranging a work programme that will keep the pupils busy and which they will find rewarding, either in itself or through your commendation of their achievements. People do things because they see some point in them and are rewarded by or for them. Much dissatisfaction with school and associated indiscipline arise from the fact that these necessary conditions are feebly satisfied or not satisfied at all. Apart from looking critically at the nature of the educational task and the extent to which teachers make it directly rewarding, it is valuable to allot at least some time (in some situations a lot of time) to issues quite outside the ordinary curriculum which are more urgent for some young people than the topics inside. For some pupils this leads legitimately to a radical reconstruction of the curriculum, so that it is made to consist of relevant problems in the perspective of the learners.

Knowing and using pupils' names is one of the best ways of aiding good discipline. On the positive side, it gives each pupil status as an individual person, which is more highly motivating than being treated as a nameless member of a crowd. In relation to unhelpful behaviour it allows the teacher to admonish named individuals and prevent the erosion of the sense of responsibility. It is worth using names even if one has to use a name chart until this can be dispensed with, and even if one can master only a proportion of the names—for example, where many classes are taught or where a class is seen only infrequently. It is better to know some names than none, and to make occasional mistakes in using them (which can be corrected in a good-humoured manner) rather than not to be seen to be trying to use them. The avoidance of anonymity is one of the most practicable steps in developing good relationships, and yet a surprising number of student teachers make very little use of names. When one visits a student who has a fluent mastery of all of the names in a class the difference is most striking.

Whatever is said about immediate disciplinary strategies, there is no escaping the fact that long-term preparation and understanding count for more. The young teacher whose education has given him broad attitudes, varied skills and knowledge, and a sympathetic approach to other people generally, has an inevitable advantage. Those who have not had a flying start in this way must cut their losses and start at once to build up intellectual, social, and practical skills on the basis of existing strong points. There is scope in teaching for a certain amount of play-acting—indeed, it is a useful subordinate skill—but the teacher's own personality and mentality, partly at least a product of education, determine the main character of his disciplinary as of his general pedagogic success. *Le style, c'est l'homme.*

The control of behaviour

A great deal of advice about discipline tends to be either rather general in character (perhaps difficult to refute and difficult to apply) or else highly specific (genuinely applicable in one situation but not easy to apply or justify in general). There is at least one disciplinary system which is rooted in a definite view of behavioural control and which generates very specific strategies for different situations. Its theoretical affinity is with the doctrine of behaviourism and it is most explicitly and vividly expounded by Clarizio (1971). Clarizio's examples are American and remind one of differences in national context, but the practical advice is readily translatable across national boundaries. The five procedures discussed and exemplified are: 1 reward, 2 modelling, 3 extinction, 4 punishment, and 5 desensitization.

1 *Reward.* Although the importance of reward may seem obvious, there are many schools and classrooms where the observer would have difficulty in spotting the rewards. He might indeed be impressed by how much children will put up with in the absence of reward. It is

easy to take schooling for granted and assume that habit or duty must keep the children working. If any pupils make life difficult the teacher may be still less inclined to reward them—even when they happen to do exactly what is wanted on some occasion. For some pupils life is (in the old saying) more kicks than halfpennies. Failure to reward what is wanted can be accompanied paradoxically by regular rewarding of exactly what is not wanted. This typically takes the form of giving attention to bad behaviour. Even if the attention is in the form of admonition or abuse this may be a better reward than nothing for some pupils.

'Dedicated professionals that we [teachers] are,' comments Clarizio, 'we would probably not show up for work if we were not reinforced by dollars.' What schools and teachers must devise is a 'reinforcement menu' for pupils—that is, a good list of rewards from which one can select to reinforce good behaviour when a child achieves it. He mentions tangible rewards—like toys, puzzles, comics, special access to popular facilities—and social rewards—like verbal commendation, a favourable note to parents, or a post of special social responsibility. Obviously it would be necessary to have different menus for children of different ages and in different circumstances. One of the defects of schools—perhaps worse as one moves into the senior ranges—is their overestimation of the idea that learning is its own reward and failure to develop reward systems, particularly for the great majority who cannot be expected to go forward into the professions or even be encouraged by their parents to see much point in school.

If a certain kind of behaviour is to be established quickly then it is best rewarded every time it occurs. Once the new pattern is more or less established it can most readily be made long-lasting by being rewarded only occasionally and irregularly. Since achievement is itself rewarding it may be worth while having visible charts of individual or class progress, and not resting content with verbal comments on progress. Since some things are harder to work at in any case, it may be worth having contracts or agreements with the class that, when certain specified work is done, the pupils may go on to another activity that is more popular. Devices like these are commonly used in a sporadic fashion, but they could be exploited systematically. Learning must be worth while by mature standards, but it must also be worth the pupils' while to pursue it. *They* must feel that it is worth while. There is no necessary question of doing everything only for specific reward, for many activities remain self-rewarding, but a policy of more frequent, varied, and specific rewards would give much educational endeavour a motivational underpinning which it demonstrably needs. Where learning problems are most serious—for example, with very slow learners or very badly behaved children—it is all the more urgent to reward scholastic progress or signs of improved conduct.

Approval is one of the most convenient kinds of reward, but it has to be the right kind of approval in the right circumstances. A young child might shamelessly enjoy the teacher's public commendation where an older pupil would be pained. The older pupil might appreciate the same commendation in private, or a subtler public commendation that identified him clearly with his peers and not as any kind of teacher's pet. It is necessary to remember, too, that approbation varies with the approver. A teacher who is known to be sympathetic and helpful, or who bestows other benefits (helping with games, visits, etc.) must count for more than the approver whose tokens are only verbal.

2 *Modelling*. The last point leads naturally into the theme of modelling—the tendency of young (and old) to learn from the models of behaviour presented by others, and particularly presented by others who enjoy special prestige or respect for specific reasons. Clarizio suggests the following as factors that influence the potency of a model—competence, status, control over resources, past helpfulness, similarity in some measure to the person influenced, support from other models modelling the same attributes, and the extent to which the features modelled seem important in the social context or aspirations of the person influenced.

It is important with modelling as with reward to think about the values and outlooks of the pupil's peer group, for the peer group ranks high on the last three potency factors listed above. The teacher who wants to be successful should try to tap the power of the peer group as well as modelling competence and helpfulness in his own dealings with pupils. The deviant pupil with high prestige in the peer group can be a threat to the teacher's endeavours, but much deviancy is tolerable. Teachers sometimes seem to envenom the sting of deviancy instead of drawing it. Of course, some deviance is intolerable in relation to prevailing circumstances and has to be more drastically dealt with, whether psychotherapeutically or punitively. If a pupil 'shows off' a bit too much or slightly oversteps the usual bounds of behaviour it seems desirable to facilitate a return to normal, if at all possible, rather than a process of escalation. If the pupil then chooses escalation he invites a harder lesson.

3 *Extinction*. Whereas reward and modelling are ways of creating behaviour patterns, extinction is the name given to a technqiue of getting rid of an established pattern, even if it is not permanently extinguished. The technique is to withhold all rewards from the undesired behaviour, including the reward of attending to it. For

example, a pupil might be in the habit of telling tales or of coming too often to the teacher's desk. Extinction technique would require that the teacher ignore the child as completely as possible—just not see him. Or, if a class was very noisy as it was about to be dismissed, extinction technique would require the teacher to stand paying no attention until the noise died down. He would then immediately commend their quietness (even if it had supervened by chance) so that they were rewarded for good behaviour where they had been ignored for bad.

It is clear that this technique would not take one far by itself. There are too many countervailing forces. The undesired behaviour may be reinforced by peer group approval or by sources outside the school. The disruptive effect of the behaviour may be too much for the teacher to ignore. As already indicated, a single reinforcement of the behaviour may sustain it for a long time, whereas a brief period of ignoring may produce no quick result. None the less, extinction may be useful as a subordinate technique—combined, for example, with positive reward for any good behaviour and isolation of an offender from immediate reinforcement of his bad behaviour (perhaps by changing his place in the classroom or even putting him in a 'foreign' class for a spell). The most immediately practical lesson of extinction for the ordinary teacher may be to beware of reinforcing bad behaviour by excessive attention, even if the attention is critical, and of failing to make good behaviour definitely rewarding.

4 *Punishment.* Where extinction aspires to ignore undesirable behaviour, punishment is the infliction of pain because of the behaviour. The deterrent effect of scholastic punishment may be greater if it is administered early rather than late, and if it is administered in one strict dose rather than a succession beginning mildly and increasing gradually in severity. Since punishment most clearly marks out what is disapproved, it is important to make equally clear what behaviour is approved. Otherwise, discrimination learning cannot so readily take place. Harsh punishment is liable to act as a negative model, so that pupils dislike all that the teacher stands for. Excluding an offender from the class for a limited period, particularly when the class work would be otherwise rewarding, may be a suitable punishment in some cases. It can also be useful to develop punishments that are to some extent sanctioned by the class in relation to an agreed programme of work or conduct.

It is possible here only to allude to the philosophic problems that arise in connection with punishment, for they are complex, but it is important to recognize at least that it is a disputed area. There are no simple solutions. Apart from problems of philosophical justification, punishment is a theme that arouses strong emotions, which can be strikingly aggressive both in sympathy with and antipathy to the notion of punishment. One person may feel that all punishment should be replaced by appropriate 'treatment', while another feels that an individual's autonomy is insulted if he is not punished for misdemeanours which he committed both freely and in knowledge of their wrongness. The area of punishment is one in which human barbarity and human sentimentality readily well to the surface. Punishments inflicted by other people are classified as punishments while one's own inflictions are seen in a different light.

People find it easier to express their feelings about punishment than to justify them. They may feel that it is a necessary deterrent, but stumble over the fact that it may be either deterrent or non-deterrent, and may even be an incitement to further wrong-doing at the first opportunity. They may feel that wrong-doers ought not 'to get away with it' but have difficulty in weighing the satisfaction of retribution against possible worsening of the proclivity to offend. A common argument is that the offender feels better for being punished, in the sense that the slate is wiped clean, but one wonders sometimes whether the offender really feels better than he might have under some alternative treatment, and whether the slate is entirely wiped clean. The notion of the punishment fitting the crime is a catch phrase with considerable currency, but it is not clear what is meant by 'fitting'. If what is meant is a punishment justified by the offence, the question of what constitutes justification is the very question at issue.

The concepts of punishment and penalty are related in a confusing way. In some contexts either term might be used. 'Well Jones, you know what the penalty/punishment for that is; I'll expect your extra exercise on Thursday morning.' Penalty perhaps suggests more strongly the existence of a clear public rule which even an offender sees to be justifiable. Punishment perhaps suggests the infliction of some pain or disadvantage by way of retribution at the instigation of some authority (teacher, headmaster) who has wide scope to manufacture rules and appropriate punishments in situations as they arise. To object to a penalty (where the relevant offence had been committed) would be to object to the rule itself. To object to a punishment after committing an offence might be to object to a rule, or it might be to object to a particular individual having so much discretion to treat one drastically without clearly justified rules. But, while one always smiles at the old saying about 'This hurts me more than it hurts you', it does correspond to some genuine situations— where a teacher acts drastically and painfully with genuine concern for the long-term welfare of his pupils. This has to be taken into account as much as the more pathetic opposite extreme of the exceptional schoolmaster who simply enjoys beating little boys.

While the young teacher must consider these issues, he will not solve many disciplinary problems by discussing them with pupils. Discussion may be useful sometimes, but most problem situations call for prompt and just action, not for philosophical reflection in the midst of the battle. The action will normally be admonition, redirection of attention and effort, moving a pupil to another place (inside or outside the classroom), or consulting with the regular teacher about what would best be done. Corporal punishment is not a direct practical question for the student teacher, although it may be of indirect consequence in a school where regular teachers use it extensively. The tide of educational history moves slowly away from the whole idea of corporal punishment, because it is doubtful how far it achieves its alleged aims, because it is a bad advertisement for education, and because it can be such a violent insult to individual autonomy. None the less, it is easier for those furthest away from difficult classes of children and young people to air such arguments. And a comparison of different national attitudes and practices soon reveals how parochial critics can be, with no sense of the significance of custom nor of the educational atrocities that can survive the disappearance of corporal punishment (for example, communal socialization and systematic indoctrination).

5 *Desensitization*. Pupils who are aggressive and disturbing are liable to worry teachers more than those who are timid and quiet, but the proper management of more inhibited, anxious children can be part of a successful programme of class discipline, and desensitization may be relevant to such cases. It is the technique of reducing anxieties by accustoming the anxious person first to a very mild variant of the class of phenomena that causes the anxiety, and gradually extending this habituation to more powerful examples. Thus, if a young child was frightened about going to school, he might be encouraged with suitable rewards to go through a gradual programme, beginning perhaps with getting up for breakfast in good time, then going to the bus stop, then making the journey to school, then approaching the classroom, entering it, and staying in it. The secret lies in having an appropriate hierarchy from events or objects creating least anxiety to those which are most difficult for the individual, and in approaching the most difficult via a suitably graduated series of efforts. If a person was frightened by the idea of being interviewed for a job, he could be given reassuring information, allowed to try a mock interview, taken by a friend to see where the interview would be conducted, and perhaps introduced to someone like himself already employed by the appointing firm, before undergoing the real interview.

The anxious pupil may be too compliant, sensitive to criticism, cautious, dependent, self-disparaging, and assiduous in avoiding attention. Direct commendation may be painful to such a pupil, partly because it focuses attention on him, partly because the praise may conflict with his poor estimation of himself. The teacher's commendations have to be more subtle and indirect and he has to remember that the brisk admonition suitable for the more self-assured pupil will not do for the more anxious. Although the problems of the over-anxious are more easily overlooked, attention to them contributes to the general good spirit of a class, particularly through their sense of the teacher's general competence in appreciating important differences.

The five means of controlling behaviour just discussed—reward, modelling, extinction, punishment, and desensitization—seem highly relevant to practical discipline. They may seem to represent too instrumental a view of education, but that is no valid objection, for all teachers are instrumental shapers of behaviour. The behavioural approach just outlined differs only in its explicitness and its systematic character. It is based on the idea that, since you are going to control any way, you might as well do so efficiently. The reservations that one might validly entertain are different. One is that teachers simply do not control many of the strongest reinforcers of behaviour, and, at least in the worst cases, have limited power compared with that of the family and society. The other is that successful discipline depends as much on the wisdom, justice, and subtlety with which a system is applied as on the system itself. But these qualifications apply to all methods of discipline. They are certainly important.

Discipline, learning, and motivation

This chapter has attempted to explore deliberately the theme of discipline so far as it can be detached from neighbouring educational problems. One does not want to be evasive by suggesting from the beginning that disciplinary problems are really other kinds of problem. None the less, almost every turn of the exploration reminds one that the neighbouring problems are part of disciplinary problems in the long run—the problems of devising curricula and methods that are felt to be useful and interesting by the various main categories of learner, of making school life more rewarding in personal terms for the pupils and not just theoretically rewarding in relation to educational principles (although that is important too), of bridging the inevitable gaps between what young people feel to be 'real' and 'relevant' and what their mentors are trying to make real and relevant (reality and relevance are not static).

The abilities to read, count, and get on with people, are fundamental. So is the ability to do a job eventually that is materially and personally satisfying. Such a specification is already quite complex in its implications, and is not met for many young people in the education system. But many additional specifications fight for a place in the sun—longer schooling or more higher education, this group of subjects or that, more educational technology or more personal counselling, more religious education or less, more freedom or more discipline. It is in the nature of education to be controversial as a topic, but, in any given time or place, teachers have to cut through the web of arguments and pursue a practical policy most likely in their eyes to benefit the young people being educated. Good discipline depends largely on how far teachers and schools contrive policies that are justifiable, varied, and decisive for those whose education depends on them. Good discipline stems from good educational policy. Even the student teacher responsible for a limited section of work in a limited context can profitably ask whether his objectives are those that are most justifiable in the circumstances and whether he is pursuing them in a varied and decisive manner in relation to the particular pupils in the class.

The beginner cannot know at once what it is reasonable to expect from pupils. Even as this knowledge comes with experience, one must be ready to insist on still higher standards upon occasions, and on others to abate one's demands. High expectations encourage high performance, provided the expectations are within reasonable range of the learners. The regular teacher may think sometimes, 'I could have told him the class would not manage that', but, on other occasions, 'I would never have believed he would get them to do that.'

Beginning teachers should not really be exposed to situations of indiscipline at its worst, but some are so exposed ('They've got to start some time'?) and it may be useful to add a special comment on this problem. Some of them see this as a special challenge and doggedly cope as best they can, sometimes motivated partly by consideration of the misfortune of children who have not learned how to benefit from learning. The more difficult the situation, the more vital it is not to stand on one's incipient professional dignity, but to consult the regular teacher or any other person in the vicinity whose help may seem worth having. Where pupils have long persisted in bad habits of behaviour and negative attitudes to learning, lowering conventional scholastic sights is an important strategy. The nominal programme may have to be set aside until one slowly establishes a line of communication, possibly based on themes that are sufficiently alive in the pupils' own lives.

It is difficult for teachers to persist without the reward of pupil response, but it may be easier to do so if the probability of low reward is recognized. One has to be rewarded by one's own achievement of persistence. It is really a game for the tough and flexible rather than the gentler variety of humanitarian. It is desirable to talk freely with friends about the problem. It may be necessary to write the practice off as a bad experience and look forward to others that will be more normal and tolerable. If things are beyond these remedies or palliatives, one had better see a tutor about getting out of the situation. Only some teachers, in any case, are ever cut out for the toughest teaching assignments. For those who persist, the watchwords are coolness, honesty, consistency, consultation.

Where disciplinary problems are of a fundamental kind that cannot be readily solved, psychological and social understanding can help to make them at least slightly more tolerable. For so many children their whole education has been a lesson in failure and it takes great restraint and perception to try and ease this burden of failure off their backs and begin to substitute something, however simple, that will give a taste of success. The deeper the problem, the less likely is a single teacher to be able to answer it very fully, but even small beginnings are worth while—not succumbing to the angry or punitive comment that surges from one's irritation, (although anger can sometimes carry a humane message), tactfully commending achievements which may be very small, creating opportunities for the pupils to choose activities or topics for study instead of sticking to some prefabricated blueprint, helping someone to find the elementary basis he lacks even if he is well past the stage when this basis is normally supplied (for example, learning to read in secondary school).

Discipline is one of those topics that stretch away in all directions. No net of discussion catches all the disciplinary fish. One can only hope to have caught some. The topic has at least been given a priority which teacher-trainers are sometimes alleged to deny it. It should be possible to turn now to wider questions of teaching method without constantly having to rehearse their disciplinary aspect.

The teacher's skills: objectives, humanity, motivation

4

This chapter concentrates on three skills—clarifying objectives, interpreting humanitarian ideals and methods, and motivating learning. A great many immediately practical points have now been made about the teacher's skills and it is time to look more systematically at what was traditionally called teaching methods or what some might call more grandiloquently theory of teaching. The term 'teaching method' has sometimes fallen into disrepute because it may seem to suggest that there is only one way, or very few ways, of teaching a particular thing, whereas common experience suggests that the same goal may be achieved by many diverse methods. There may also be an apparently prescriptive tone which offends the individual teacher's sense of his own autonomy. However, since this suspicion about the term 'method' seems somewhat exaggerated, the word will not be studiously avoided in this section.

It is essential to distinguish what a brief discussion of teaching methods can and cannot do. It cannot instruct teachers in the detailed knowledge and skills necessary for specific teaching tasks—teaching infants and juniors to read, or other pupils to do mathematics or appreciate literature. Each specific area of that kind has its own extensive literature (see Appendix B). Nor can a general discussion abstract some general teaching formula that will *guarantee* that any specific teaching will be so much better, for general principles, however valid, always depend on practical interpretative skill for their final efficacy. What can be hoped for is a broader and better balanced perspective on the character of teaching problems, a fuller awareness of the considerations that should be taken into account in facing any teaching problem, and a more developed sense of priorities. Any teacher can probably think up his own examples of educational achievements being limited by narrow perspectives, neglect of important relevant factors, and misjudging of what things come first.

Clear objectives

If challenged to apply the test of priorities to the teacher's own skills one is at once reminded of how difficult this exercise is, even for an experienced person. When so many skills are potentially relevant none should be dismissed or improperly diminished in importance. However, it is tempting to give precedence (a) to skill in formulating objectives that are both identifiable and justifiable, and (b) to skill in helping children to be and feel human in the best sense. It should not be thought that the former skill can be taken for granted. Even leaving aside the question of justifying objectives—which leads naturally into quite difficult areas of discussion—one finds quite often that a young teacher either is not at all clear what he is trying to achieve, or else that his teaching is inspired by conflicting objectives. The first situation can arise where a lesson copies mechanically the superficial format of someone else's work, without analysis of the nature of that work. The second can arise in a similar way, but with elements copied superficially from several different models—for example, the model of the regular teacher, the model of the tutor's advice, and the ideal model of the student's own conceptions. The dilemma cannot be avoided, but it can be recognized with a view to sharpening awareness of what one really does want to aim at.

Giving precedence to the desirability of clear objectives is suggested probably by the only too human tendency to take the line of least resistance. One of the notorious examples of this is the tendency to fall back on the patterns of teaching experienced by oneself as a learner. Hence the almost universal (and, of course, partly valuable) phenomenon of using methods suitable for academics with pupils who will spend almost no part of their lives in academic pursuits. A practical solution has to be pursued by moderating rather than abandoning the modes of the teacher's own education. The latter is impossible any way, unless one envisages treating prospective infant teachers like infants (which has sometimes happened) or middle school teachers like pubescent boys and girls.

Personal experience as a pupil is not, of course, the only dangerous fall-back position. General theories of education, ridiculously reduced to slogans, are another escape route from the fresh, practical formulation of objectives. Examples are easily found—school tradition, child-centredness, progressivism, activity, creativity, relevance to life, academic achievement. All of these concepts are potentially fruitful, but it is easier to go for the slogan and the tokens

CARNEGIE LIBRARY
LIVINGSTONE COLLEGE
SALISBURY, N. C. 28144

of allegiance to a philosophy than to keep translating it into teaching programmes that are openly justifiable even to a detached observer. Nor should one be fooled by those who purport to be anti-theoreticians. Their strategem is to pour so much scorn on all theories of education that one is supposed not to notice that their views on education are also theories. Doubtless they would go on to claim that their theories are at least grounded in fact rather than fancy, but this itself is a theoretical claim. The moderate improvements in public education that have taken place in the past century have been hard won by people striving beyond the apparent 'facts' and against the conservatism of established practice.

The dangers just outlined are the dangers of accepting any panacea, whether of one individual or of some general theory of educational success. It is another dilemma that can be noted but not escaped. The desire for panaceas is perennial. It is partly an urge to simplify the variety of human aspirations under one clear goal, and partly a parallel urge to economize on effort by means of some standard method. Two directions of this urge are particularly striking in the history of education. One is what might be called the encyclopaedic urge—the notion that all essential learning can be wrapped up in some encyclopaedia, library, text-book, or learning system. It is the attempt to tie education down in some finite physical form. The other direction of simplification might be called the apostolic or discipleship urge—the selection of some individual as a kind of educational *guru*. Rousseau, Arnold, Froebel, and Dewey are examples from the past. Readers can conjure up their own list from contemporary celebrities. This apostolic urge is the attempt to tie education down to some finite personal form. The utility of these two simplifying tendencies is obvious, but each has to struggle both for a place alongside its own generic rivals and with the infinite variety of life constantly blurring the neatness of any system whatsoever. The only practical policy is to explore systems and persons that seem to connect with one's own teaching problems, while remembering that wisdom is not a monopoly.

The practical teaching skill of envisaging reasonably clear objectives is one of the most sophisticated skills, for it draws on one's entire human understanding—psychological, social, intellectual, and specifically professional. Some of the most immediately relevant considerations have been discussed in earlier chapters. What must be added here is a reminder of certain balancing problems that exist wherever teaching objectives have to be determined. Three of the most important balancing acts could be represented systematically in the following way:

The child and the culture   (a) The best educational objectives are those suggested by a child's present capacities and pleasures and most closely related to the immediate social sphere in which he lives or is likely to live.   (b) The best educational objectives are those suggested by the human cultural inheritance as a whole, to which everyone should be initiated regardless (so far as possible) of incidental social and psychological circumstances.

Freedom and constraint   (a) Individual autonomy is so important that one should fight constantly against the constraints that tend to develop within educational institutions.   (b) Appropriate constraints are implicit in the very idea of education, and, indeed, in the ideal of freedom, for freedom necessitates a choice among different and incompatible freedoms.

Tradition and change   (a) The main purpose of education should be to initiate children into the knowledge, skills, and attitudes that are of proven value rather than to attempt to change society radically with the inadequate tools of even the best education system. (b) What suited the past or suits the present will not necessarily suit the future. Children should receive an education positively oriented towards perpetual social reform.

These antitheses haunt educational thought and practice. They invite closer definition of the terms typically used. They invite speculation about the nature of men and societies. They provide a forum for the expression of individual temperament and for rationalization of allegiances that may really rest on deeper and hidden grounds. But these tempting fields of enquiry must be eschewed in the present context, where relevance to teaching practice is the priority. In this context the antithesis chart has practical importance as an identification and correction device. It provides three dimensions on which to make crude assessments of one's own and other people's overt or covert style of pursuing educational objectives. It is then possible in one's own case to consider whether, in any given situation, it might be justifiable to correct an excessive tendency in a particular direction.

Is the beginning teacher too preoccupied with his own parcel of culture? Is he a kind of defective cultural sub-station failing to transform on to the lower voltage suitable for younger learners? Or is he riding a wave of child-centredness which makes him underestimate the materials and systems that are necessary to give pupils their human and educational entitlement? Is he one hundred per cent for freedom and en route to classroom chaos, or does he err on the authoritarian side and require practice in gradual relaxation? Is he pleased with himself because the school is glad to see him fitting in with its traditions, or is he a thorn in the headmaster's flesh because of his callow enthusiasm for reform and change? Most will not be at any of these rhetorical extremes. The typical area for possible modification is in the middle, where the teacher gradually moves toward the compromise that best suits his ideals, his temperament, and the expectations of colleagues.

A second practical deduction from the above antitheses is that one is not called on to emphasize the same kinds of objective all of the time. Part of the subtlety of good teaching is to make room for different kinds of objective at different times. This not only helps to do justice to diverse kinds of value, but also helps to motivate learners by the diversification of their programme and by communicating to them that one respects different values and abilities, and by implication different kinds of people. One is not simply a single-minded pusher of limited pedagogic wares. In practice the more limited policy has been commonly pursued in schools. Lessons have been: too long; too unvaried; too inactive for the pupils; too lacking in even minor opportunities for pupils to exercise choice within the framework of established studies; too much taken for granted with little attention to stating, let alone 'selling', their justification; and too heedless of wide divergencies in learning capacity and of the profound frustration that is built up by having to persist, perhaps for years, in an activity which produces failure and opprobrium. Many current developments in formulating teaching objectives and methods are helping to lighten this dark side of the picture. The beginner might use the check list of possible deficiencies in assessing his own teaching.

A third practical point is that a teacher's personal list of priorities —the list that sums up the general tenor of his teaching aspirations— has to be altered for occasions when it is clearly not working. This is easier to point out than to act on, even although it is one of the most obvious requirements of practical teaching. One of the commonest versions of fixed priorities is the assumption that certain skills must have been, or should have been, acquired at an earlier stage when, in fact, they clearly have not. Many junior children and some secondary school pupils have not really mastered even the fundamentals of reading skill. Although this skill is not an ordinary priority for later stages of schooling, it must be made a special priority for the appropriate pupils, and, indeed, requires systematic provision in some schools. The case of reading is particularly important, but learners of any subject at any level may include some whose most urgent scholastic need is to get hold of the planks that are missing from their learning platform.

There is often a need for a still more fundamental application of the maxim, *reculer pour mieux sauter*. That is where a child or a class is overwhelmed by some problem or concern that makes all ordinary school learning trivial or distasteful in the learner's perspective. A minor example is the child who has just had some exciting experience and cannot settle down until he gets it off his chest to the teacher or somebody else. While it is hardly practical to spend all day listening to trivial stories, it can pay dividends to create at least limited opportunities for pupils to unburden themselves in an informal way. A more serious example is that of the child who has some really grave problem on his mind, perhaps associated with a disturbed family background, and who cannot really give his mind to ordinary school work. There are no stock remedies here, but clearly a need for sensitivity, helpfulness, and restraint on the part of the teacher. Then there is the most difficult case of all, where all or most of a class may come from grossly disadvantageous environments, and where even a teacher's permanent teaching objectives have to be different from what they would be in average circumstances.

Humanity

These examples may begin to suggest why, in this discussion of priorities, the ideal of clear objectives is coupled with the idea of humanity. Humanity involves respect for both what people are and what they might become. It is not, therefore, just a matter of being 'soft', but rather of subtlety in judging when more can be expected of people and when social and pedagogic pressures should be abated. The beginning teacher probably does right to keep his expectations high, even if he may be rapidly driven to correct them realistically downwards. But there is no reason why he should not at the same time be ready to show a benevolent interest in the pupils' special concerns as well as expecting them to take an interest in his scholastic demands.

Reference has already been made to the importance of interpreting a humanitarian approach with due regard for the fact that pupils are younger and less experienced than teachers. The fact that some senior pupils are almost as old as the youngest teachers, and that some pupils are more experienced in certain things than their teachers, does not alter the general truth. Disparity in age and sophistication certainly does not mean that teachers should be condescending, but it does mean that they should not expect children to respond socially with the maturity of adults, and should not expect that complete mutuality of response that is possible mainly among coevals. They should not expect a social reward from the children for benefits bestowed. This is not to say that they will not get such responses or rewards, nor that maturer responses should not be encouraged when they do occur. It is only that the teacher must be independent. The beginner, perhaps not feeling very independent in respect of his teaching skill, can be betrayed into a too explicit effort for the favour of his class.

Having commended this detached humanitarianism, one must go on to say that it has its own dangers. One is the danger of the teacher expecting too much of himself. A conscientious young teacher might assume personal responsibility for all that happens under his teaching. Without going back on the idea that he ought to accept responsibility for his own teaching, it is practically important to be realistic about the shared responsibility that characterizes all complex human situations. The pupils themselves must be treated as responsible so that they may learn to be responsible. This means that their contributions, whether for good or evil, to the classroom situation must be identified and commented on. Other circumstances beyond the teacher's control are responsible for some of what happens and there is no call for each individual to shoulder the sins of the world in too literal a sense. The practical outcome of extreme conscientiousness of this kind could be sheer inefficiency. Overwhelmed by the vastness of the conceivable problems, the teacher might fail to get on with some extremely modest but perfectly practicable teaching task.

Another way in which humanitarianism can get out of hand and defeat its own ends is where it is imagined that teachers and schools can put to rights the deepest defects of society. Teachers and schools must certainly contribute to social amelioration, but in terms of the tasks they are genuinely equipped to undertake, and not by imagining that a teacher's efforts can be a substitute for stable family relations, good housing, regular employment, and the general moral tone of a society. Where schools as institutions can make a substantial compensatory contribution to the defects of other social institutions (such as the family), this has to be organized on a sufficiently large and systematic scale. Even where large compensatory education programmes are mounted, they have many stubborn difficulties to face. This highlights the limitations that are bound to be set to any single teacher's efforts to improve society. The individual contribution has to be planned modestly—sometimes in terms of concrete help with basic learning skills, sometimes in terms of trying to get young people to feel like human beings and to develop their understanding of what being human can mean.

Of course, no single individual, however varied his sympathies and talents, can represent all that is meant by being human. What even the limited individual can do is try to keep alive the idea that there are different worthwhile paths for different young people to follow. At the same time he must make clear that some paths should be trodden by all because they are of such fundamental importance. There is bound to be dispute about what is really fundamental, and probably some tendency for each specialist to want his pet enthusiasm to be squeezed into the fundamental category. However, few would deny a place to reading, writing, counting, and whatever activities or studies help young people *immediately and directly* to understand themselves and to deal with the personal problems of their own lives.

To teach with conviction one must teach as if the lesson of the moment were all-important, and yet the mature teacher keeps in mind that not only that lesson but his whole teaching may have little relevance for what a pupil feels to be his real life. Some of the hollow justifications offered for, and little difference made by, many courses of instruction confirm this quite clearly. However, the fact that the horse may not drink does not mean it should not be taken to the water. Even where a pupil does not do well in a particular study (despite genuine effort) the teacher of that subject probably helps his own work most by (i) trying to keep his subject open for the pupil, even if at a modest level of interest, (ii) trying to sustain interest in the pupil as a person, regardless of his limited achievement, and (iii) trying to show appreciation of the pupil's possibly greater achievements in other areas.

One of the commonest sources of unconvincing teaching—teaching that does not seem to connect at all with anybody's life, let alone the pupils'—is lack of conviction in the teacher himself. Such a teacher may use defective methods, but his real trouble may be that he is a kind of intellectual fraud. The material of his teaching has little significance for him personally. He may profess literature or history or science with an eye to bread-winning, but spend little or none of his private time in the pursuit of these studies at an adult level. Even among the more academically inclined of experienced teachers it is striking how often they must avow regretfully that they 'have not had much time for serious private reading in recent years'.

There are often understandable reasons for this, and, of course, it would be ridiculous to expect everyone to be equally enthusiastic about every aspect of a professed subject. Nevertheless, the beginner trying to formulate sound objectives, and to teach his material with a sense of humanity and perspective, should not underrate the importance of genuine enthusiasm, that is, enthusiasm springing from actual commitment to a study, and not just whipped up for the lesson of the moment. Teachers may have to simulate and dissimulate for some of the time, but this should be only an occasional and *faute de mieux* resort.

Motivation

What has been said about clarity and humanity in defining and pursuing teaching objectives leaves many aspects of these ideals unexplored, but at least some practical points have been suggested. The theme of motivation is central to educational method and constitutes a natural extension both of the immediately preceding sections and of the discussion of discipline in the last chapter.

The first thing to be said about the motivation of learning is that there is no one simple problem but rather a variety of complex problems. Motivation is not just a question of turning up some short-term stimulus to action—zealous exhortation, menacing scowl, promise of early reward, threat of dire action, or titillation with ephemeral novelties—even although these have their subordinate place in the motivational armoury. It is rather a question of having a wide understanding of learning and development, of temperament, intelligence, and socialization. It is a question of selecting appropriate objectives in the first instance for any group of learners in particular circumstances, and of devising detailed programmes of work that lead by well-judged stages towards the achievement of the objectives. Many imagined failures of motivation are really failures in choice of aim or in programming the necessary learning.

Since choice of objectives and programme must be influenced by things like age, sex, general ability, temperament, social background, school atmosphere, and local and national cultural norms, as well as by the nature of the specific learning task envisaged, it is clear that successful motivation must mean successful assessment of these factors and appropriate deployment of educational resources. There is no simple formula pointing unerringly to what makes assessment successful or deployment of resources appropriate. One can only chart some approaches that may be practically helpful if developed along with the practical study of the psychology of learning.

A common approach to motivation is via the concept of psychological needs. The idea is that, if one knows what needs children have, they can be educated by appealing to these needs. Just as a child can be kept physically alive by the supply of suitable food and drink, he can be kept psychologically alive and thriving by meeting his needs for things like security, affection, and varied sensory and intellectual stimulation. But this psychology of needs has been challenged. It can be argued that any need is based on an assumption about what is desirable or valuable. Needs are not simple biological facts. Even the apparently basic need for a minimum of food and drink is based on the assumption that survival is an absolute desideratum—an assumption challenged by those who risk their lives in warfare and hazardous sports, or who choose martyrdom or suicide. If one argues that the latter are abnormal or not really commendable, this just emphasizes that the argument has moved from the factual to the normative level, to a discussion of what should be rather than of what is.

If this is so for the minimal need to survive, which one can agree is at least a widely if not universally held aspiration, how much more relative do needs become as one moves from the needs for food, water, and rest, through the needs for affection, exploration, or varied stimulation, to the most highly relative needs of all—of the cultivated musician for Bartok or Messiaen, the educated parent for a university for his offspring, or the gourmet for Russian caviare and the best champagne. What are necessities and what are luxuries? For some, spartan living is a kind of indulgence; for others sumptuous living may be a penance, a bore, or a cause of premature death.

And yet, while recognizing the evaluative character of needs—ranging from aspirations which most people share to others which are more relative and open to dispute—the very fact that at least some values are almost universally shared, whether overtly or covertly, is relevant to the teacher in his attempts to influence behaviour. There is some utility in the idea of a hierarchy of needs, the higher ones being most estimable as ideals to which we aspire, the lower or intermediary ones necessary to keep us going along the road. The admirable lecture, but the welcome coffee-break. The inspiring recital, but the social stimulus of a friend's company. The dirt and sweat of putting the garden in order, but the friendly commendation from a passing neighbour. The noble academic ideal of study for its own sake, but the welcome salary cheque or vacation to sweeten one's labours.

If teachers applied these considerations to their pupils as readily as all adults apply them to themselves, then learning motivation in schools would be increased. The teacher is certainly expected to create needs in the sense of new values, and not just to blow gently on some limited set of needs that are supposed to pre-exist, but, as has already been suggested, higher values can often be encouraged by at least humouring lower ones. The scholastic demand is to be tempered by the expression of human sympathy, the intense spurt of work by the period of relaxation, routine labours by the occasional novelty or treat, preoccupation with school affairs by concern for the pupils' out-of-school world, consideration for adult convenience by consideration for the personal world of the young.

Since motivation is partly a matter of enticing others to share one's own values, it is important, as suggested in the last section, that any values to be communicated should be at least sympathetically appreciated by the teacher. (One can easily imagine values—religious or political, for example—to which a teacher might not subscribe, although he appreciated why others did subscribe to them.) But it is only practical to recognize some of the difficulties. Different values are to be won with different degrees of difficulty, depending on the nature of the value itself, the circumstances in which it is to be communicated, the limitations of the pupils, and the character of the teacher's own subscription (or non-subscription) to any value in question. As any of these indexes tends towards the negative pole, motivation is bound to be more difficult—a fact recognized in the history of denominational schooling.

It is only practical, too, to recognize that neither teacher nor pupil can subscribe fully and actively to all of the cultural values on offer. Teachers tend to be expected to achieve, or pretend to achieve, more than is possible. But there must be selection and limitations. Equally, few pupils can be lovers of poetry, keen sportsmen, facile mathematicians, ingenious students of science, avid readers of history—all rolled into one. One step towards sound motivation of learning consists in accepting willingly what people are, or have a chance of becoming, good at. Beyond these limits one wants to tempt learners rather gently if they are not simply to have their noses rubbed in failure.

Commercial advertisers are freer and readier to plunge down the motivational hierarchy for stimuli likely to catch, if not sustain, public attention. Their motivational appeals are familiar—sex, hunger, thirst, social self-assertion or acceptance, novelty, and humour. The teacher cannot allow himself the advertiser's blatancy, nor has he the simple test of success represented by the business man's sales chart. Yet he might sometimes take a leaf from the advertiser's note-book, even if, like the reliable manufacturer, he must sustain the quality of his product and not just trick people into having it.

A beginner may think vaguely that he alone must motivate pupils' learning, but habit and custom are among the most powerful motivational forces, particularly if they are associated with any sense of achievement. A new broom approach may destroy more motivational power than it creates, although new brooms are obviously much needed in some circumstances. Certainly the new teacher, even the new student teacher, has a chance, because of his newness, of establishing his own set of expectations. The sooner and more definitely he establishes these, the easier will subsequent motivational problems be.

But it is only realistic to recognize that there are schools and classes where inferior work habits are already strongly entrenched, and the student is likely to have to struggle as best he can within an unsatisfactory situation. The best plan may be to concentrate on making plenty of work for the pupils—work which will demand real effort but give a good chance of success. The opposite policy to be avoided is a predominance of expository teaching, which keeps the teacher busy and the pupils free for boredom or mischief.

The place of examinations in motivating learning always provokes controversy. Although some teachers attack examinations vehemently the vast majority would probably value examinations for their potential motivation to achievement. It is difficult to take seriously those who like to imagine the complete abolition of examinations, for it is impossible to imagine seriously a world in which people did not assess one another in some way or other, and motivate one another in virtue of such assessments, however diversely made. The serious question seems to be how the manifest ill-effects of known assessment systems can be reduced or abolished, so that people are motivated to do things that are really worth while. Some possible ways include (i) more varied kinds of assessment, (ii) more opportunities for re-assessment, (iii) more attempts to reduce rather than increase the emotive steam that precedes and surrounds examinations, and (iv) more positive emphasis on activities dissociated from competitive examination. These suggestions, however, have to make their way in a world which everywhere remains persistently competitive.

Another serious problem is that of motivating the slowest learners or the really badly behaved. The beginnings of a solution have been tentatively outlined, but there is no easy solution. The slower learners should have permanent scholastic provision for their special needs— groups, or classes, or schools where they are not forced into failure by the pressures of average learners, or where they can recoup earlier lost ground with a view to rejoining the average learners if they are capable of doing so. People are torn between the obvious value of special provisions and the fear of segregating any group in an inferior enclave. A compromise has to be reached according to circumstances, but systematic special provision must be a part of it.

Perhaps enough has been said about behaviour problems in the last chapter, but here too there is often a need to abate the scholastic pressures that are reasonable for average children, so that more expression can be given in some relatively constructive way to the frustrations and conflicts that support the bad behaviour. It is often desirable or necessary in the worst cases to have physically separate provision for seriously disturbed disrupters of ordinary school work. Motivation to ordinary work is blocked by sometimes tortuous patterns of motivation to behave in destructive ways.

Throughout childhood motivation can be misjudged by the teacher expecting too much or too little. There can be no general formula to solve the problem. A young child may need a respite from normal standards if he is a slow learner. But then there is a whole school of psychological thought which stresses the importance of expectation, highly structured learning programmes, and varied intellectual stimulation for socially handicapped pre-school children. If one moves to another point in the developmental spectrum—adolescence —there is the danger of expecting adult standards from young people who are at most immature adults, but also of placing childish curbs on these same young people who yearn for adult status, whatever their limits in meeting adult responsibilities. Psychological studies have deepened our understanding of all of these matters, but by filling out the detailed picture via surveys and clinical studies, not by providing facile formulae. The understanding is available, but one must take time to read and reflect and relate the various psychological analyses to one's personal experience.

Two considerations from the realm of social psychology have a direct bearing on learning motivation. One is the demonstrated contribution of parental encouragement to scholastic achievement. The other is the possibility—perhaps no more than a possibility— that techniques of co-operative instead of competitive learning among children may motivate children of varied ability to identify themselves with the enterprise of learning, to be more naturally sustained in it, as adults to some extent sustain one another by mutual assistance in work, and to succeed more in virtue of both the social stimulus and the technical aid which it may include. The fact that these are possibilities is stressed, for co-operative enthusiasts are apt to forget how people of like ability may be drawn to one another, and how the competitive pressures of society impinge upon children from an early stage, even in egalitarian societies.

The significance of parental encouragement and pressure is more definitely established, as one might expect. It is interesting that children seem to develop the so-called differential need for achievement, under parental stimulus, even from the pre-school years. There is nothing mysterious about this when one considers how many factors reinforce one another—consistent parental affection, combined with consistent high expectation, combined with consistent commendation of achievement within the home where the child spends most of his time, and where, at most, a few siblings are rivals for parental favour. What a contrast in school for the child who can have only a smaller share of attention, from a teacher and not a parent, and for relatively short periods of time!

If one accepts the psychological analysis of motivation as it has just been sketchily outlined—how inadequately in relation to human complexities—then one major conclusion is that teachers can accept responsibility for only part of the motivational burden. Admittedly, quite a large part; but not also that part that must be shared by parents, administrators, legislators, and all of those who contribute to the values that prevail in society at large. But there will always be controversy and discord over public values. This is another reason for teachers making a realistic appraisal of their responsibility, that is, an appraisal that gives more weight to valid compromises and reconciliations than to the pursuit of some fanciful millennium.

There is one fundamental aspect of the psychology of motivating children's learning that tends to be overlooked. That is the psychology of motivating teachers' teaching, and educational administrators' administrating, and educational legislators' legislating. The details of our motivational policies will doubtless vary with developmental stages, and with individual personalities, even with temporary phases in a single personality, but, if the more general psychology of motivation is applicable to children it must apply also to their mentors. The teacher must get his encouragement, his respite, his recognition, and his chance to learn and develop.

The teacher's skills: communication, resources, programmes

5

This chapter will deal with the skills of (1) communicating with pupils, (2) exploiting educational resources, and (3) programming various units of learning. Obviously, this is a division of convenience and partly arbitrary. A great deal has already been said about these themes in earlier chapters. Teaching skills are interdependent. Sound discipline and effective communication, humane teaching and skilful programming of lessons, reasonable objectives and varied deployment of obtainable resources, are all mutually beneficial—or, if badly conceived or managed, mutually detrimental. Nevertheless, the themes of this chapter are sufficiently large and distinct to deserve some special elaboration. Before embarking on these themes it would be useful to say a short word about an ancillary theme that bears on them.

Efficiency? Humanity?

Throughout all discussions of educational practice there is an underlying, or sometimes quite overt, tension between those drawn to models of mechanical efficiency and those drawn to models of open-ended human interaction in relation to teaching and learning. It can be argued against the former that even physical machines in this technological age are as notorious for their deficiencies and breakdowns as for their impressive achievements in favourable circumstances. Why, then, should one expect human learning to accommodate itself to such a model, for human beings are even fuller of surprises?

Against the open-ended model and the distaste for too specific tests of efficiency, it can be argued that teachers are not paid salaries just to interact open-endedly with their pupils. Surely there must be some specific educational outcomes, and if so, surely it is fair enough to assess the efficiency with which the outcome is achieved? Is it achieved at all? At what cost? Is there something better that might have been achieved for the same cost? Or perhaps even for less cost? And what, in any case, are these open-ended virtues that are to be taken on trust and protected from the savage materialism of the efficiency expert?

The open-ended model has a long history, but variants of it can be studied from Rousseau and Dewey down to A. S. Neill and other more recent exponents of child-centred radicalism. 'The operations of our minds', suggests W. K. Richmond (1971), 'far from being mechanistic, are energized in the blood and first break surface in the consciousness in the form of emotion. It is their *élan* that prompts the search for strategies.' This reminds one of the old and true saying that much learning is caught rather than taught. If the fire of enthusiasm is present the resources and organization will come in good time. Teachers and pupils are envisaged primarily as people living and working with one another, not as sets of interacting roles or speech codes (abstractions of the sociologist), sets of interacting 'behaviours' (the psychologist's abstraction), or sets of manpower units (as fed into the economist's computerized model).

Some detached analysts of teaching certainly seem to lack a sense of some of the less admirable by-products of their own work—a sense of how they convert autonomous people into manipulable abstractions, make or imply judgments about activities to which they have no personal commitment, and play down the function of their researches as a means of sustaining their own careers—just as fitting in with a particular school or educational authority is a large part of the teacher's means of sustaining his career. There is nothing remarkable or wrong about the existence of these features of the detached position. They are inevitable. But greater reflection upon them might help some to avoid a certain naïve offensiveness—as in those conscientious wonderings about how the results of research can be got through to the benighted teacher in his classroom. It is not surprising that teachers have their revenge by wondering how the life of the classroom can be communicated to the benighted researchers.

Probably the tension just described must be reckoned a permanent one, with salutary as well as unfortunate aspects. The high cost of education services and the competing demands of other social services, equally or more important, necessitate some respect for efficiency as well as humanity. What matters is to be clear about the goals of efficiency. It is impressive how often even sophisticated people conceive of efficiency as a kind of end in itself. But always one must ask, Efficient for what purpose? Efficiency does not mean the trappings of efficiency—systems, programmes, figures, concentrated authority, uniformity, and the rest. It means economy of effort and resources in achieving ends which are genuinely justifiable. If there is dispute about what these ends may be—which there frequently is—this dispute should not be confused with the question of efficiency in the means. And even apparent questions of means may really involve questions of subordinate ends. The roundabout means may be more educative than the direct route to a particular educational goal. One has to consider, therefore, how important (not just how economic) it is to pick up the incidental educative experiences, or whether the main goal alone should determine the means to it. The answer will be different on different occasions.

The beginning teacher probably has to derive what benefit he can from each of the models just compared. The model of free human interaction comes most easily. One tries to be oneself with others who are also being themselves. One plays it by ear, thankful for the situation already prepared by others, and for the live working models constituted by regular teachers. But then it is not quite so simple. Neither teacher nor pupil is just *one* self. Which self is the student or teacher or pupil to be? Not, presumably, one's worst self? Ideally, one's best self? Not just oneself *in vacuo*, but oneself related to a school and society which has expectations of pupils and teachers? At this point one is inevitably poised to face up to any enquiry which will clarify insight into self, other people, or society—be the enquiry psychological, sociological, economic, commonsensical, or anything else.

Communication

Like efficiency, communication is a concept freely tossed around as if it were a ball—a single, definite thing. But there are differences between communicating knowledge, attitudes, and skills; between communicating facts and reasons; between communicating verbal and practical mastery of concepts; between communicating for temporary and permanent purposes. There are differences arising from different media of communication, and differences arising from the different characteristics of the persons with whom one is communicating. There is communication *with* and communication *to*. There are questions of the relevance and the significance of anything communicated. There are questions of the context of anything communicated—contexts of particular activities, particular languages, particular societies. Anyone who wants to communicate on the topic of communication has some explaining to do.

Even so, there is perhaps a short-cut to some of the most practical problems of communication in teaching in the form of the following ten propositions, which, while provisional, have some general or systematic evidence behind them. In each case, where it seems possible, a suggestion (*) is made about the minimal relevance of the point to a beginner's teaching practice.

1 There is too much effort to communicate relatively useless knowledge, and not enough to communicate useful attitudes and skills. (Examination success before manners and morals? But, of course, what *is* useful? And how are knowledge, skills, and attitudes interrelated?)

   * One can try to give as deliberate attention to encouraging constructive behaviour, enjoyment of learning, and practical exercises of relevant skills, as to ordering the presentation of materials.

2 There is a good deal of communication of bad attitudes. (Frustration through failure? Excessive laxity or strictness? Neglect of the human aspect of things in favour of subject routines?)

   * One can deliberately avoid or correct tendencies in these directions and think of good behaviour and attitudes as constituting a legitimate and necessary objective alongside the practice of subject skills and the acquisition of new knowledge.

3 Intellectual matters are communicated too much in terms of factual knowledge—which is certainly part of understanding—but not enough in terms of practised skills. (Get them to say the 'right' thing—that is, parroting skill—whether or not they can apply their purported knowledge in fresh contexts.)

   * One can get pupils to find out more for themselves—use concrete materials, make their own notes on visits, experiments or reading, use reference books, solve problems individually or in discussion groups. Since this tends to take more time than the school system sometimes allows, it may be necessary to compromise by allotting at least part of the available time to such work. Some real learning is better than none.

4 There is more emphasis on communicating facts than reasons, on communicating the verbal form of reasons than practical competence in reasoning, and on reasoning within a narrowly defined context rather than practising the same reasoning in different contexts.

   * One can familiarize oneself with the many curriculum development projects and resources which try to circumvent these shortcomings. These try to give the teacher more concrete varied and appealing resources and more rational learning programmes, than the

traditional syllabus or textbook. However, real understanding takes time and imagination. The teacher (as suggested above) must *make* at least some time. Also, if he does not cultivate genuine reasoning himself, but treads the path of pedagogic fraud, his pupils are as likely to follow his bad as his good example. But example is not enough. Pupils must be interested in real problems (or simulated problems) which will necessitate reasoning, and allowed to develop this reasoning in discussions with one another. To reason privately and silently is a more sophisticated task.

5 There is more emphasis on communicating for short-term purposes within a scholastic context than for long-term purposes in the context of the large part of life which is non-scholastic, not to say anti-educational.

* One can bring into discussions and practical work opportunities for pupils to express and use personal knowledge and skills acquired outside of school. But one need not overstress this. Schools have distinctive things to do and there is much to be said for learning to do these well before being carried away by broader enthusiasms. Some scholastic things contribute enormously to wider social purposes. Nevertheless, even these thrive better where the teacher shows wider sympathies. Where the pupils are at any kind of serious social disadvantage, scholastic tasks will hardly thrive at all unless the teacher tempers them to the pupils' circumstances, moving sympathetically and gradually.

6 There is a predominant emphasis on modes of communicating to and with the more academically able. Sir Alec Clegg and Barbara Megson (1968) suggest that: 'In its heart of hearts this age believes that the child with a modest ability does not really count. . . . In the secondary school the substance of education, which is the development of the total personality, tends all too often to give way to the shadow, which is measurable book learning.'

* Since all teachers are, relative to the whole population, academically more able, they are exposed to the risk of misjudging the objectives and methods suitable for most pupils. They normally become aware of this problem quite early, and must simply take time to come to terms with it. At the same time, one cannot sympathize entirely with the worst detractors from academic achievement. Everyone would be worse off without the positive achievements of the academic world, and a young teacher's mind can be harmfully divided when (sometimes) his own new professional colleagues give little esteem to what he has been doing for most of his twenty years, and what these colleagues also did for about one fifth of their allotted span.

The word 'academic' does not itself distinguish what is good or bad about an academic training. The rhetoricians bandy it about in lieu of harder thinking. It would be more accurate and less demoralizing to assert that a good academic or technical basis is essential for all teaching, but that it is not enough by itself for most teaching purposes. The more arid aspects have to be trimmed away (and most young teachers soon do that—sometimes even before they have left their academic folds), the more vital aspects still have to be transformed into terms that are intelligible and appealing to youngsters, and less academic skills such as getting on with people and institutions have to be cultivated if not already possessed.

If some first slogans were to be offered to guide this transformation they might include—use simple and concrete language, attempt only a little at a time, think of illustrations and activities to facilitate understanding, and recapitulate and revise from time to time (both to strengthen first impressions and give second chances of understanding to those who missed the point the first time). These are maxims that may help to counter the speed, complexity, density, and abstraction that often characterize academic programmes.

7 Just as there is uncertainty about what constitutes usefulness (point 1), so there is uncertainty about what constitutes relevance or significance in communication. (Margaret Bryant (1972) on history teaching: 'We must replace the hectic quest for relevance with a rediscovery of significance.')

* There is no special practical point to add here. The problem tests one's whole ability to conceive worthwhile objectives and pursue them in a way that links with the present and ultimate needs of young people. Many of the official reports (Newson, Plowden, etc.) offer suggestions.

8 It is easy to forget that apparent limits in communication may be limitations of an alterable system. (The man in the next school, or the next town, or across the border, may be overcoming similar communication difficulties to one's own, but without special thought or bother.)

* The beginner must look particularly to his own systems—his behaviour, preparation, techniques—with a view to expanding not only his technical skills but his imagination. This depends on his whole education and professional preparation. More varied experience can improve perspective.

Language, the teacher, and society

The last two points to be made in this set of ten are sufficiently important and distinct to deserve a section on their own. As indicated by the sub-heading, they concern the place of language in mediating, in both directions, between the teacher and ultimately society.

9 There is more time spent on oral communication than on communication by other media, and on the teacher's oral communications than on the pupils' oral expression and exploration of the material to be communicated.

* Oral communication—or communication by speech, in case anyone should have the pleasures of kissing in mind—can obviously justify its prominent place because of its ubiquitous force and subtlety. One does well to attend to skill in speaking, difficult as it is to modify fundamental speech patterns, particularly given the shortage of speech therapists. But the beginner notoriously, and even the more experienced teacher commonly, may not give nearly enough scope for pupils to talk. Talking about and around a topic is the commonest adult way of coming to understand it and committing oneself to it. It seems likely that the same would apply to children if they got rather more chance than they do.

The beginner can ration his own talking and plan considerable periods of time when the pupils do the talking by discussion or answering questions. There should be some attempt to spread the participation in such activities, with special wariness for the quiet pupil who succeeds in melting out of the teacher's attention, and for the rumbustious pupil who must get his chance—but not everyone else's as well. Where the lesson is to be centred on some other kind of pupil activity—which may still include quiet discussion among pupils—the beginner can still take care not to restrict the active learning time by prolonging his own exposition of material or instructions.

There has been a great increase in the use of pictures, charts, film strips, radio and television programmes, school visits of many kinds, and other devices for making learning more vivid and varied. Any of these aids can be as futile and boring as a bad teacher, just as a good teacher alone can be as vivid and effective in some tasks as any audio-visual aid. One can familiarize oneself with the range of aids that are genuinely available (or makeable) and bring into use those which might support one's personal presentation and management of any lesson or project. Aids should serve a definite purpose and be relatively easy to use—two criteria not always satisfied.

10 Limitations in the teacher's (not just the pupil's) use and understanding of language are common limitations on communication.

* Some vivid and practical illustrations of this are provided by Barnes and Britton (1969). A selection of points, emerging from their detailed analysis of a small sample of lessons on different subjects by different teachers, may suggest possibilities of practical improvement in the teacher's awareness and use of language in teaching.

(a) 'Since most questions in the sample (of questions used in lessons) were closed-ended (that is, expected only one possible answer), pupils were seldom invited to think aloud, to generate new sequences of thought, to explore implications.'

(b) Factual questions predominated over reasoning questions in most of the lessons.

(c) 'Teachers talk far more than pupils can reply.'

(d) Pupils commonly have to struggle, not just with the nature of any problem itself, but with guessing what the teacher expects. The teacher does not really need the pupil's explanation, and, therefore, the explanation does not serve the practical purpose that explanations ordinarily serve. It is a kind of game, in which the pupil has to work out the teacher's personal rules as well as understanding the objective problem. Idiosyncratic expectations of this kind are a common feature of lessons. The teacher struggles to elicit a preconceived answer, sometimes brushing aside offers that have some sense even if they are not quite correct, or ignoring the evidence of senseless answers that the basic material has not really been grasped by members of the class.

(e) Barnes and Britton give a neat illustration of how a teacher (of science) accepted a nearly correct answer but with a tactful improvement of its accuracy:
'Pupil   There isn't any air, sir.
Teacher   Good. There isn't much air.'

(f) Teachers sometimes treat a re-wording of an expression as if that constituted an explanation. (What does three times six mean? It means six multiplied by three.)

(g) Teachers' language readily moves into impersonal, abstract forms which may not really be understood by children. Barnes and Britton illustrate with such concepts as 'complete in themselves' or 'tended to be', which come readily to a teacher's tongue, but are quite complex in meaning. He also gives an example which is as relevant to the learning of adult as of juvenile students. For the teacher, 'explain' means 'Make a logical statement about causes within the implied framework of the subject'. For the pupil or student, 'explain' means 'Make any statement relevant to the matter in hand'. Barnes and Britton do not take the cynical step necessary to cover those cases where 'explain' seems to be interpreted as 'make any statement, plausibly associated with the matter in hand'.

(h) One general conclusion suggested by the study of Barnes and Britton is that children should be encouraged to use language as a means of learning any subject. Language should not be monopolized by the teacher for formal instructional purposes. And when language is used for instruction, there should be some definite attempt to capture the simplicity and directness of everyday speech. There should not be a premature rush to technical formulations before the learners have understood the substance of what is to be learned.

Apart from analyses like that of Barnes and Britton, which have a very direct bearing on practical pedagogy, educational sociology has popularized what might be thought to be rather obvious, namely that there are important differences in the characteristic modes of speech of people from different social classes. The prolonging of schooling for all and the concern with educational equality have sensitized people to the problem of teachers with one set of language habits and associated conceptual assumptions communicating with pupils whose language habits and conceptual assumptions may be different. The teacher's language is a subtly elaborated instrument for self-expression, explicit reasoning and social control. The language of a manual worker's child may be more direct, concrete, and limited—handicapping him at school, not only in superficial aspects of expressive style, but in power to master conceptual learning.

It is easier to note and chart the phenomenon than to know what practical conclusions are to be drawn, apart from points already made in the discussion of Barnes and Britton. It is another of those cases where the practising teacher seems to be faced with a dilemma and then left to make what he can of it. He is expected to compensate for linguistic impoverishment, but respect the positive cultural values of the impoverished environment; to believe in compensatory education, but not to dwell on the continuing detrimental powers of bad social or family environments; to make known educational values more universally and equally available, but to be slightly ashamed of the fact that these values are tainted with the dire suspicion of being 'middle class'.

Many young teachers may feel happy to leave these problems in the realm of theory, but others will be sensitive to their practical importance in any policy of maximizing educational opportunity. There is no easy practical advice to be given. It is valuable to develop some sense of the variety of social circumstances and at least to appreciate that one's own social assumptions, right or wrong, are not the only ones. But it is also practically important to try and identify what specific things can be done to help any learner simply as a particular human being and not as a notional unit in some stereotype of a social class.

Eric Midwinter (1971), in an essay called 'Children from another world' about Educational Priority Areas, offers some realistic advice for teachers in these most gravely socially handicapped areas. In EPAs, even more than elsewhere, teaching 'can be testing to the character, threatening to the person, and wearying to the spirit. . . Teachers should not expect too much from their efforts. . . Aim and content should come before method. . . Enlist the assistance of the home. . . Teaching in educational priority areas is not for everyone. . . Young teachers of the socially disadvantaged must rely on themselves.' Areas of social disadvantage obviously call for extra sensitivity to disparities between teacher and pupil language codes, and extra effort to help children and young people develop the ability to express and analyse their own problems by discussion.

Language has so many functions—communicating and eliciting information and explanations, expressing and exploring problems, expressing personal attitudes or cultural assumptions, inviting or excluding the participation of others, elaborating trains of logical reasoning or venting emotions, affirming and questioning, raising and dashing hopes, evoking pride and shame. Teachers, like others, slip in and out of these various uses of language, leaving behind them a trail of human effects that may be intentional or unintentional, and (in either case) admirable or disastrous.

It is particularly easy to imagine that the impersonal or objective material of a lesson is the real lesson. All these other linguistic functions may come in—but only incidentally and relatively in-effectually. This is just what the student of language use must question. Typically the linguistic incidentals are themselves the core of what really influences pupils—the throw-away notes of encourag-ment or discouragement, good or ill humour, condescension or respect, confidence or diffidence, cynicism or faith. The teacher's personal manners and style, expressed in many ways but particularly through modes of language, *are* the lesson as much as the contents of the lesson notes, the work programme, or the class text.

This discussion of the importance of language in teaching requires three corrective notes to conclude it. The value of encouraging much more talk by pupils has been stressed, but pupil talk, in the form of irrelevant and distracting chatter, can be a problem for the beginning teacher. He must make clear what are occasions for discussion and what are occasions for silent work. Training in silence or in listening has its value as well as training in purposive discussion.

The importance of making allowances for social and linguistic handicaps has been stressed, but the vast majority of pupils are not gravely handicapped in these ways, and a considerable minority have social and linguistic resources equal to the teacher's—indeed, greater in some cases. If some teachers in some circumstances have to concentrate on what was earlier called the downward transformation of educational voltage, others in other circumstances find themselves challenged to raise their own voltage to the pupils' level. Teachers can tarnish their image by rubbing the noses of the slow learners in scholastic failure, but also by giving very bright children a sense of facile and contemptuous superiority.

Finally, the importance of trying to examine one's teaching language in a broader perspective has been stressed, of watching out for the linguistic clues to assumptions and attitudes that may deserve questioning. But this reflective activity has to be separated from the on-going job of teaching. Otherwise, action will falter. One's main language patterns are an integral part of social interaction. They are not bits and pieces that can be stuck on or pulled off. Reflection on the teacher's language is reflection on his whole social being. It is not, as is commonly imagined, just reflection upon verbal fluency or stylistic elegance, but on the nature of one's mind and personality. Hence the common hypersensitivity to criticism in this area. Self-consciousness for better long-term understanding has to be offset by a certain unselfconsciousness in doing the practical job.

Resources

The teacher's most important resource is himself. That may be the conclusion that has to be drawn from all that has now been said about controlling pupils, defining objectives, acting with humanity, motivating learning, improving techniques of communication, and understanding the profound and ubiquitous influence of individual language habits. Another major resource, the school itself, with its particular equipment and materials inside and particular physical environment outside, its particular set of people and particular set of public expectations, tends to be taken for granted.

There is much that simply has to be lived with. These more static resources may tilt one's endeavours in directions which are feebly justifiable in a broader view. Alternatively, when more favourable, they may give a more valuable and powerful direction to teaching than any teacher could match by personal effort alone. Particular sylla-buses with particular sets of books, apparatus, or equipment represent resources that are still more static than one may like, but which are susceptible to modification by teachers from time to time.

Most schools have much more audio-visual equipment than they once had, but organizational, time-tabling, or technical problems, may dull the brightness of the educational technologist's pedagogic vision. There is the problem of generating detectable educational benefit from audio-visual devices other than the benefit of relieving the monotony of other modes of learning. The potential is impressive, but, as with all techniques, human effort somewhere is necessary to generate the actual educational effect.

Student teachers are usually encouraged to study and use all kinds of audio-visual aid—the chalkboard, charts, illustrative objects, models, radio or television, film strips or films, and tape-recorders. Despite the jokes that may be made about audio-visual enthusiasm, it seems only sensible that beginners should take the trouble to try out these aids, for they can make learning more varied and vivid, and less exclusively dependent on verbal abstractions. Not that a picture or tape-recording is not also an abstraction—but at least it is of a different kind, with distinctive virtues, particularly fullness of detail in illustrating general points.

The effective use of aids depends on thinking in detail about all of the practical requirements for effectiveness. Is there space on the class wall for one's brilliant pictorial illustration? Is it possible and permissible to stick suitable tacks into the surface? Can the class really decipher what they are supposed to? Is there a suitable point, plug, and length of cord, for your projector? Have you an alternative strategy if your audio-visual aid breaks down for unforeseeable reasons? Can the class be blacked out if that is necessary, and can you control the pupils as the room is darkened? Can your aids be deployed within a minute or thereabouts, or is there a danger of disorder while you slowly unwrap yourself from a large map? If an exhibit is to be handed round the room, will this take everyone's attention from what you have to say? And is your precious picture or object fit to be handled by miscellaneous youthful paws?

Apart from these practical matters, it is also important to allow sufficient time both for the audio-visual display, and for the activity or discussion that is to elicit or confirm the point of the display. It takes only a late start, a minor interruption, a technical hitch with the material, to find that there is time only to have the display and no more. The audio-visual element is left high and dry—a pleasing change from work, but subserving no substantial learning. This, of course, can apply to traditional verbal exposition, but the latter can be more instantly modified, whereas many audio-visual presentations require a certain length of time to serve any purpose at all.

There has been a great expansion in the supply of packages of learning materials—reproductions of pictorial and documentary evidence bearing on particular themes. This kind of aid is obviously highly flexible both in its contents and uses, ranging from sets carefully prepared and tested by national bodies like the Schools Council, through various commercial packs to the kind of *ad hoc* collections that teachers and pupils can make for themselves. Practical problems that have to be kept in mind include cost and possibly rapid wear and tear of such materials.

Advantages include the potential vividness, variety, and intellectual stimulus of the materials, and also, the stimulus to the teacher to refresh his own knowledge by continuing to seek out source materials and not rely only on second-hand text-book summaries. Of course, where new and varied materials are part of some large scale project, like those in science, mathematics, and the humanities, there is always the danger that the dead hand of system will reassert itself. There is no final resting place in the continual balance between the effectiveness of vividness and variety on the one hand and of system and routine on the other.

The use of the chalkboard is, of course, part of the stock in trade of any teacher. Its convenience is obvious—for confirming, illustrating, summing up, holding material before the eye, trying out and correcting new learning, focussing attention, receiving contributions to the lesson from pupils, supplying clear (or obscure) models to guide the pupils' individual work. The first practical problem is surprisingly difficult—it is to write or draw sufficiently clearly with chalk and to deploy the writing or drawing in the limited space actually available. If the board is to be used both for developing a systematic plan and for recording miscellaneous incidentals (spellings of words, etc.), it is probably advisable to divide the space with a line from the beginning. If there is not enough space for this, then the incidentals have to be curtailed or rubbed out after serving their immediate purpose, or else the systematic chart has to be developed or presented by some other device (perhaps prepared on a large sheet of paper if this seems worth doing).

One teacher suggested that beginners should not turn their backs on the class to work at the chalkboard until they have secure control of the class. The teacher facing the chalkboard is certainly a classical cartoon situation for pupil mischief. And those illustrations of the ideal teacher coolly facing the class while he writes sideways on the board may outrun the physical and psychological flexibility of some beginners. A practical policy would be to avoid writing for more than a very short period, unless the class is busy with its own work, and to interrupt longer periods of chalkboard work by frequently turning round and addressing points or questions to the class.

Those teachers who practise and develop skill in neat writing, vivid pictorial illustration, ingenious drawing of maps, charts, and diagrams, and confident exploitation of chalkboard space, add greatly to their immediate pedagogic stature and effectiveness, but the many whose talents in these directions are somewhat limited should still persist in search of at least simple legibility, system, and vividness, even if they cannot attain the heights of chalkboard aesthetics.

Books, paper, and pencils or pens, are fundamental resources, and yet it is often a struggle to get what is felt to be necessary, and to ensure that pupils do not forget the books and jotters they have, or break pencil points, or otherwise veer between remissness and sabotage. These apparently trivial matters can wreck the best educational intentions, sew distraction through the class, and encourage poor standards of behaviour generally. Therefore, while teachers should always try to be ready with constructive strategies (spare paper, pencils, etc.), pupils should be left in no doubt that one is 'not amused' by carelessness which is damaging to class activities.

Books are of fundamental educational importance because of the practical and intellectual power they put in the hands of those who can use them. They can fire the imagination (of course, for good or ill), guide people in practical matters, systematize knowledge, or chart the range of human life and thought that constantly defies system. They are available in enormous variety, catering for every human study and interest and for every stage of sophistication. They ought to be the teacher's friend, for appropriate ones in the hands of pupils do the teacher's work for him. The school or local library can be, and often is, a major resource for the teacher of any subject. But good wine needs no bush. Why should one even bother to utter these points?

One answer could be taken from the annual figures for local authority expenditure on school books. There is a wide disparity between the most and least generous expenditures. (Even in Scotland, where per capita expenditure on books and educational supplies generally is higher than in England, the 1969–70 estimated figures for school books ranged from £1·52 to £2·59 per pupil in the main cities, and from £1·01 to £8·91 over all authorities.) Another answer is that books, like teachers, are quite costly, and there are always pressures to cut costs.

Finally, many teachers themselves do not have a sense of the varied purposes of books. The teacher of literature may underrate technical literature. The science teacher may underestimate the exciting wealth of books that portray the social and human ramifications of science and overestimate his familiar expository texts. The teacher of juniors may overstock the class library with books with a particular kind of appeal, while other equally important kinds are under-represented. Even the student teacher can improve his work by helping children to get hold of a wider range of supporting literature than may be represented by the stock texts. The effort of compiling background booklists for different purposes, of searching through libraries, bookshops, exhibitions, and catalogues, is worthwhile for its extension of one's command over one of the teacher's most central resources.

The last resources that will be mentioned here might be called people and places. While regular teachers are obviously in a better position to organize class visits out of school, or invite interesting guests into the classroom, student teachers may often have the regular teacher's co-operation in making an educational visit, or be allowed to share in a visit organized as part of the class's ordinary work. The same arguments apply here about ensuring that some clear benefit or lesson is derived from an educational visit. This is a matter of preparation, good organization, and subsequent review of the experience, although these steps do not require a heavy-handedness of style which turns an occasion of extra liveliness into a bore. Indeed, many visits or special experiences are best left to speak for themselves, but one should have a clear view of what kind of experience is intended on any given occasion.

Whatever the intended purpose of any visit, or of any other extracurricular activity (sport, school clubs, musical events, etc.), the teacher may reap an important incidental benefit—of getting to know children out of the necessary restrictions of the classroom setting. Neutral ground can encourage more freshly human exchanges —provided that there is not such looseness and unrealism in the planning that a less desirable 'freshness' comes to the surface, of the kind that has brought disrepute on some visits abroad.

Programmes

Many examples have been given of how good teaching depends on recognizing the factors that are relevant in a particular situation and then keeping a balance between them. In programming or planning a lesson, a project, or a whole course of work over a term, one of the main balances that has to be struck is between the importance of good instruction on the one hand and the importance of creating active learning opportunities on the other.

This particular balance is so fundamental that debates about it pervade the literature of education. Even in the long centuries when few concessions were made to any child-centred ideal and children were expected to accommodate themselves (or else!), there were always occasional voices raised by some teachers to remind themselves and others that the harsh winds of academic learning have to be tempered to the shorn lambs on the classroom bench. From Rousseau in the mid-eighteenth century to Dewey in the early twentieth the importance of giving more scope for the educational potential of the child's own nature was increasingly emphasized, with many back swipes at the bad old authoritarian days.

Through the twentieth century the child-centred ideal has established itself very slowly and on a limited scale—more in primary and less in secondary education, more in America and less in Europe (but with some academic counter-reaction in both continents, particularly in the last decade or two). It is interesting, therefore, that an American psychologist (J. S. Bruner) is one of those who have become associated with a more recent emphasis on the importance of a theory of instruction as well as a theory of learning. Bruner envisages such a theory as one which

1 'should specify the experiences which most effectively implant in the individual a predisposition towards learning';

2 'must specify the ways in which a body of learning should be structured so that it can be most readily grasped by the learner' (and good structure means structure which (a) simplifies information, (b) generates new propositions, and (c) makes a body of knowledge more manipulable);

3 'should specify the most effective sequences in which to present the materials to be learned'; and

4 'should specify the nature and pacing of rewards and punishment in the process of learning and teaching' ('punishment' presumably meaning aversive control, not retributive punishment).

It could be debated whether there was such a thing as *a* theory of instruction or whether the requirements specific to particular kinds of learning outweigh any common elements. One might consider whether any common elements are so general in character that they amount simply to the old-fashioned teaching principles that dominated the scene before the child-centred era and have dominated much, even most, of it during that era. The teacher is now sometimes exhorted to be a 'manager of learning'—a phrase that tries to do justice to the teacher's positive instructional role, as envisaged traditionally or by Bruner—and at the same time to the child-centred ideal. The latter envisages children initiating much of their own learning (even if the school and teacher provide a stimulating and controlling setting), making their own discoveries (even if these are contrived), and pursuing a more varied set of activities, which may happen to subserve traditional purposes (associated with preparation for adult life) but which may be accepted as worth while solely because they are felt by the children themselves to be worth while and are not seen by the teacher to be positively harmful.

The beginning teacher faces the two aspects at once in the ideas of the lesson and the project, the former tending to be thought of as something one gives (however much pupil activity may be skilfully worked into it), the latter as a set of activities on a theme, elaborated by the pupils themselves (however much the teacher may give the lead, set the limits, and top up the ideas supplied by the learners). It is perhaps most helpful to good teaching to think of it as a balance between these two, rather than to imagine a sharp division. The teacher's role is central in either direction. In one direction he is contriving specific learning sequences predetermined by him, with as much pupil activity and participation as may facilitate that learning. In the other direction he is contriving learning sequences of a more open-ended kind, but still with quite definite objectives, namely the encouragement of variety and initiative, and also the development of knowledge and skills, even if the scope of these is not so precisely predetermined.

One trap for the beginner's project is that of planning it like a traditional lesson, except that the plan includes various predetermined enquiries, activities, and products, which are subtly 'sold' to the pupils as if they were the pupils' own. The teacher can show all the trappings of project method with hardly any attempt to apply the original project ideal, namely, taking time to let the pupil formulate the problem and ways of enquiring into it. The project can even come to mean the physical products of the project—the models, the class frieze, or whatever they may be. The visitor is then invited to 'come and see our project'. But the product is not the project. The project is the activity of enquiry and the learning that accompanies it.

The practical problems of lessons and projects are similar in many ways. They are the problems of defining at least the broad scope of one's objectives, giving clear instructions, organizing time, resources, and activities within the actual constraints of the school programme. It is always worth asking, What will I do if I do not get as far as I hoped, or if I get further than I expected, in a given unit of time? It is not possible to predict progress with great accuracy, but it is possible to have contingency plans for these two common eventualities. It is useful to take time to make clear to pupils what the programme of work is, whether for a lesson or a longer series of learning units. Children, like adults, are better to know, at least roughly, where they are going, how long they have to get there, and what the main stages of the journey will be. It is also worth reviewing progress occasionally, both for encouragement and guidance ('Now we have done, A, B, C . . . Good. The next thing we have to do is . . .').

The problem of distributing time is matched by that of distributing attention, typically among many pupils or groups of pupils. Like the time problem, this is one that invites solution by systematic analysis and correction of wrong tendencies. It is not like problems of the teacher's basic voice or personality, which can be improved only by a longer programme of self-understanding and effort. The teacher can resolve in advance that he will direct so many questions to each part of the class, that he will concentrate for a time on those who are most reticent, that he will have all pupils attempt all questions by getting them to write brief answers to a quick set of oral questions.

He can plan that certain groups will need all of their time to do written or other work, while he gives his personal attention to other groups which need it. He can switch his attention among slow, average, and fast learners. This means that it is often necessary to think of parallel programmes of work, and the division of classes into diverse working groups is now a commonplace. While the point of group work is obvious, it seems essential to concentrate on economy of teacher effort if it is to work successfully. One of the criteria for good grouping must be the teacher's power to manage it. Better to have two or three groups that can be managed than four or five which may be justifiable on the pupils' capacities but not in terms of manageability.

Similarly, in working out a policy for marking or commenting on pupils' work, or for dealing with pupils' incidental enquiries, it is essential to judge what is practicable and not just what would be ideal in ideal circumstances. Commenting on work and answering enquiries are completely desirable in principle. That is not being questioned. But work is still valuable if only some of it is assessed or commented on in detail. And the teacher is not the only source of answers to enquiries. The teacher who exploits any device he can contrive to make pupils self-reliant in these matters is both encouraging a valuable attitude and skill, and freeing himself to deploy his attention on larger rather than more trivial matters.

One would press the argument even further in some circumstances, where it may be defensible to neglect some desirable activity completely, even in the absence of second line alternatives, because another objective requires one's complete attention at that time. Some beginners, for example, could afford to concentrate for a period on teaching their class that poor general conduct is not to be tolerated, even if other scholastic objectives are temporarily subordinated. Some lessons are given by means of the teacher making clear what absolutely matters to him—what he will go to war for. If constructive and co-operative conduct does not seem to matter, the pupils' conclusion may be, Why bother then?

The same argument can apply in a different direction. It is often felt that examinations are what really matters in practice, and that anything else must be subordinated. Schools make a great deal of their competitive successes, whether scholastic or sporting. A teacher may feel that he has no alternative but to accept these values. He has a passing sympathy for other objectives, but decides to be 'realistic'. Without necessarily quarrelling with the 'realistic' approach, one can question whether *some* of the fervour expended on preparation for examinations might not be transferred to doing things which were felt to be worthwhile, regardless of examinations. One wonders whether such a policy might not even contribute to improved work in examinations. The present concern is not to debate this issue, but only to refer to it as a case where a teacher, if he felt that way, might make clear to his class that he expected some work from them that was not directly geared to examinations. This would be a small blow struck for what a teacher might feel to be genuine education.

In case the previous paragraph should seem too much of a slur on examinations, one might go on to say that any teaching programme must include some means of assessing its own achievement. Assessment is part of the teaching programme, clarifying what has been achieved and what has to be achieved, and contributing to the motivation of learners to surpass themselves or to make good their deficiencies. Although examinations and tests are modes of assessment that come to mind at once, teachers make casual or considered assessments all the time, whether they are commending a detail contributed by a pupil to a class lesson or commenting on the progress of the class over a term's work. The teacher who makes prompt, explicit, frequent, and discriminating, comments on the work of the class and of its individual members, provides part of that sustaining guidance and encouragement on which learning depends.

Some interesting forms of programming pupils' work will not be discussed in detail here, because they are themes on their own, or because they are not central to the typical work of a beginning teacher. The very phrase 'programmed learning' has come to be used in a narrower sense to refer to units of learning, analysed into a specially graded series of expository units, each requiring a response by the individual learner. Detailed analysis of the learning sequence and the requirement of a response at every stage by every learner represent a logical extension of what ordinary teaching tries to do but cannot do completely. But programmed learning in the narrower sense has its problems too, and these are discussed in the relevant literature.

Team teaching is another idea in the air. It might be illustrated roughly with an example. If one has ninety pupils and three teachers, each teacher can be given thirty pupils and sent away to get on with the job. In the team teaching alternative the teachers would work out a joint programme for all of the pupils. They might set half of them to work in a library, and tutor the rest in groups of fifteen. One teacher might give a talk to the ninety, while the other two prepared other units of work. All might share some common experience and then do work based on it in three classes of thirty. The method has obvious possibilities of variety and impact, but also special problems of planning and co-ordination.

And a third kind of programme is that of gaming or simulation. Just as the young child may be helped in his counting and social skills by playing at shops, or an older child develop an elementary sense of property deals via Monopoly, so it is possible to devise games which simulate, for example, social, historical, or geographical problems. Different groups of pupils may be set to justify various possible policies among which some historical character had to decide, or to justify diverse contemporary transport policies on the basis of geographical and other evidence. It obviously requires considerable definition of the scope of the problem, availability of resources, and working out of the rules of the game, in order to make a success of simulation exercises, but beginning teachers sometimes have success with such devices used on a small scale.

Apart from general programmatic ideas like the three just described, beginners will obviously take pains to find out and study any of the specialized teaching programmes that are relevant to their work—audio-visual language courses, the many systems of teaching the fundamentals of reading, various science and mathematics programmes, and many others. These programmes present resources and work plans that surpass what the unaided teacher can do for himself. Without any sacrifice of autonomy or responsibility, the teacher must study the relevance of such material to his own purposes.

Assessment of teaching and learning

6

'The brutal research fact is that in spite of over 2,000 studies we have no objective criteria of what constitutes teacher competence . . . a teacher may be effective with one group of children and ineffective with another . . . efficiency may be modified by the physical, social and cultural environment in which the teacher operates.' This summary comment by Edith Cope (1971) may bring consolation or satisfaction to some and despair to others, but teaching will continue to be assessed and it is as well to take a closer look at the problem.

Some underlying problems

There are three fundamental questions about assessment. What exactly is it that one is trying to assess? What is the purpose of making the assessment? And what means of assessment will achieve the purpose most efficiently with a minimum of harmful side-effects? Each question offers plenty of scope for disagreement in particular cases, and further confusion arises from failures to recognize or avow that there are different kinds of question. Critics commonly attack assessment systems for their demonstrable imperfections or evil side-effects, ignoring or playing down the fact that the typical practical aim must be to make improvements rather than leap to perfection. The more radical may make a pretence of opposing assessment in any form, while surreptitiously substituting their own covert assessment system. The psychometric enthusiasts may be carried away by the legitimate enough concern for technical improvements, while ignoring the fact that all assessment must take place within some system of social values, which goes beyond simple metric functions, which requires great subtlety for its just appraisal, and which is quite likely to be intrinsically controversial.

The main purposes of assessment also are threefold—(a) selection and guidance, (b) motivation, and (c) the maintenance of publicly recognized standards which at least partly stabilize the drifting sands of diverse values and assessment procedures. It is conceivable to challenge all of these purposes on the ground that they *can* represent some kind of manipulation of people to conform to, or take for granted, certain fixed values or procedures. However, while few—or, more accurately, few in those societies accustomed to extensive freedom—would seriously quarrel with the value of continuing rational reappraisal, this does not argue for failing to act for the best with the best available means when practical action is called for at a particular time.

As already suggested, assessment and its typical purposes are built into the pattern of human life. Even a would-be anarchist inescapably proposes standards, albeit those of chaos, and assesses people and action in terms of them. Since it is so difficult, if not impossible, to stick consistently to pure chance and whimsy, the anarchic principle tends to drift back into expediency, a quite different thing, for this is the principle of putting one's own convenience first. Expediency is obviously a practical policy up to a point. The difficulty arises when different interests clash and one is driven back at least to some provisional standards which facilitate practical action by people in conflict.

The reason for stressing these underlying aspects of assessment is to eliminate from the beginning those general misunderstandings that can be eliminated, for, even then, there is still plenty of room for debate. All that has been said in previous chapters underlines the variety of things embraced by the concept of teaching, and consequently, the difficulty of knowing what is being assessed on any occasion when teaching is supposed to be assessed.

The purposes of assessing teachers or teaching are also varied: (a) to decide whether a candidate should be admitted to professional training in the first instance, (b) to provide student teacher and tutor with a means of guiding the former's progress; (c) to decide whether a student teacher has reached the minimal level of professional competence which justifies his being admitted to the powers and advantages of professional status; (d) to guide the tutor in formulating a fair letter of reference when the young teacher applies for a job, and appointing bodies in deciding whether a particular candidate is the best for a particular post; (e) to sustain critical appreciation and discourse among all teachers about the practical standards of the profession and the means of attaining them; (f) to further research into the more detailed analysis of teaching activities, in relation to pedagogical, economic, or other specified purposes.

While purposes (a) to (d) are those that touch the young teacher most directly and practically, this chapter will endeavour to set these in the wider context of the last two purposes listed.

Since young teachers reading this are likely to have obtained admission to a course of professional training, little need be said about the assessment procedures for such admission. The remarks of Morrison and McIntyre (1969) about the characteristics of teachers in general are at least somewhat reassuring. 'Teachers tend to be well-adjusted, emotionally stable, objective and sociable people.' In detailed characteristics there is more difference among different groups of teachers than between teachers as a whole and the general population. Teachers 'may be more inclined than most to behave in conformity with the social pressures which they experience'—but, of course, the significance of this can be variously interpreted.

There is one practical point about assessment that may agonizingly face a very few young teachers, just started on their professional course. What if one rather quickly assesses oneself as having made a wrong choice in starting to train as a teacher? The sensible course is to discuss the problem with anyone likely to be able to help. It is important, although difficult, to make sure that any such feeling is not a product of temporary circumstances that have a chance of changing for the better. Sometimes there is a difficult problem of resolving a conflict between parental expectations (which, even in these supposedly permissive days, occasionally exercise maleficently constricting rather than beneficent influence) and the young person's actual feeling about the professional course.

The more difficult the problem the more necessary it is to find one or more mature persons who can help one to identify the objective features of the problem and the objective means of solving or alleviating it. The problem may be centred in the teaching situation but, as with many apparently technical problems in a human context, there may be other personal problems that are the real root of the trouble. These, as well as the ostensible problem which may seem to be the cause of a minor crisis, require an airing to sympathetic ears.

Self-assessment and teaching notes

There may be some place for the kind of assessment and guidance which is virtually imposed—like the street corner barrier which forces all but the most perverse and athletic pedestrians to keep to the pavement for their own good at that point. Even such a barrier has an element of self-guidance in so far as it might be considered to represent people's better assessment of their own long-term interest, despite the objective constraint on the passing inclination of particular persons to prefer the more suicidal path. Certainly self-guidance seems preferable to anything that is imposed, but the central question is always one of justification. If something is seen to be justified it is less likely to be felt as an imposition. There may be an exception where something is recognized as justifiable but also as uncongenial—particularly if someone else rubs one's nose in the justifiability without showing sympathy for the uncongeniality.

These considerations are relevant to one of the traditional devices for facilitating self-assessment and self-guidance by student-teachers—the teaching record, or teaching practice notebook. It is a device to encourage planning of teaching in some systematic and purposeful way, and to facilitate subsequent comment on the degree of success achieved by any plan. It is also a record of work done and of valuable points observed in the course of any teaching practice. It should not be an elaborate ritual presentation to pacify some tutor's schematic enthusiasm, nor should it be a set of scruffy and scrappy jottings to publicize some student's lack of serious effort. It should be an intelligently and clearly kept work-book, on which further teaching and further discussion can be based.

When the author, not too long ago, prepared some notes on this topic for a small group of graduate student teachers they were as follows:

Teaching practice notebook: a few suggestions

1. A record that will be clearly meaningful to you or to a tutor. Not *too* detailed or extensive. Such that you could use it easily to comment on your teaching experience at the end of the practice.

2. Factual observations.
   (a) The children—their age-range, general and special abilities, variations in personality and ways of behaving, interests, likes and dislikes.
   (b) Their learning—the books and materials they use, the pattern of their time-table, useful or successful techniques that strike you, special difficulties in learning.

3. Lessons taken by you.
   (a) Brief record if it is a lesson taken without special preparation.
   (b) If it is a prepared lesson, use some systematic way of setting down the plan, preferably on one page only. (On reflection, one page seems unduly constricting. The intention was to emphasize structure rather than a mass of detail.) Consider the examples given by tutors, but use your own

discretion too. Some points to include might be:

    (i) Brief statement of specific aim.
    (ii) Materials you will need. (Attempt variety. Avoid complexity.)
    (iii) What will the class do?
    (iv) How will you check their success in doing it?
    (v) How will you bring the lesson to an end?
(Estimate the time you expect to give to each main part of the lesson. All kinds of things tend to make one take longer than one expects. Perhaps worth deducting 5 minutes from the total time to allow for miscellaneous losses of time. If, contrary to the above, you do finish earlier, consider what you might do. A quick revision of some points? A round of class questions? A brief discussion of some topic of current interest to the class?)

(c) Perhaps each day jot down a comment on your teaching. What features of your prepared lesson went well and invite development? What things, if any, would you do differently another time?

Obviously these notes are just one example and would not be the best for all students or all circumstances. Some tutors like two parallel columns, one containing what might be called the content or substance of the lesson or project, the other the materials, apparatus, and techniques that will be deployed at each stage. Many students use their notes to record expository material rather fully—for example, a section of historical exposition which they may have compiled specially for a particular lesson. This is often necessary, for even an able honours graduate in history has many gaps in historical knowledge. A danger associated with this necessity is that the lesson (in the old saying) smells of the lamp. It is not a natural part of the teacher's mind and, as he constantly turns to his notes, the pupils are less likely to take it into their minds.

There is no formula for making either teaching or teaching notes meaningful. Both tutors and students vary in liveliness or listlessness, earnestness or casualness, promptness or dilatoriness, demanding or facile standards, humanity or impersonality. But there are many middle ways and no reason why most tutors and students should not find one that they can follow without loss of self-respect. Those at the extremes must have a harder job to justify themselves. The notebook should be an aid to professional reflection, to the development of what is best in practice and the elimination of what is worst.

Despite the emphasis given traditionally and again in this book to the importance of knowing clearly what one is trying to do, teaching is rarely the smooth implementation of a plan. Since flux is so typical of the classroom scene, it is not surprising that flexibility has become a cliché for the necessary response. The practical thing is to strike a balance between systematic planning and sensible improvisation, between the creative work of teaching and the analytic work of assessing what succeeds or fails, between being oneself and looking at what one is being. There are different times for each phase of learning to teach, for the phase of action and the phase of reflection.

Improvements come piecemeal. A young teacher could attempt to draw up a check-list of general teaching practice objectives and periodically give himself a 'health check' with this diagnostic instrument. A sample list is given in Appendix A, but, even as one writes down such a list, its limitations declare themselves. One is reminded, perhaps usefully, of one or two areas deserving special attention, but also that the attention will not develop just from looking at a systematic list. It is rather like the shopping reminder board on the kitchen wall. You can stick pegs opposite sugar, potatoes, toilet paper, and cinnamon, but forget the cinnamon (or, worse still, the toilet paper) through the distraction of having coffee with a friend or attending to some crisis created by the kids.

Part of anyone's self-assessment is an automatic reflection (except for the most thick-skinned or most withdrawn) of the assessments implied in the responses of pupils and colleagues. The summary by Dr Kathleen Evans (1965) of the likes and dislikes of pupils, as indicated by research enquiries, always seems to suggest a sensible orientation for teachers.

> Children like teachers who are kind, friendly, cheerful, patient, helpful, fair, have a sense of humour, show an understanding of children's problems, allow plenty of pupil activity and at the same time maintain order. They dislike teachers who use sarcasm and ridicule, are domineering and have favourites, who punish to secure discipline, fail to provide for the needs of individual pupils and have disagreeable personality peculiarities.

It is a tall order, but at least something to think about as one tries to improve teaching competence.

Morrison and McIntyre (1969) are sceptical about the extent of students' capacities to observe what happens in classrooms. 'Without some training in this complex skill, which is very rarely given, students, accustomed as they are to a very different role in classrooms, are unlikely to take a sufficiently analytic view to notice and reflect upon any but the most dramatic of classroom incidents.' Their proposal 'to utilize psychological insights in increasing practical skills' seems sensible, although some might still feel sceptical about how much psychology really has to offer in practical terms.

Two relatively new forms of teaching practice that could be considered to give more weight to self-assessment are (a) indirect supervision and (b) microteaching. The first is the system whereby the student is not systematically visited in the classroom by his tutor, but instead reports his classroom experience in a later discussion session with the tutor. Strictly speaking, what is new is the emphasis on this technique rather than the technique itself, for most tutors presumably discuss the students' general experience as well as seeing particular lessons taught. There may be another novel element in the implication that what matters is encouraging the young teacher to express and work through the problems of teaching as personal problems, rather than as technical problems to be solved by mechanical adaptation. There is a good point here, but it can be met without tutors diminishing their own salutary contacts with the student in the classroom environment as well as in the tutorial study or office.

Microteaching will be discussed in the next chapter, but, briefly, it is a system of practising a particular teaching skill (say, the skill of asking more questions, or of giving more commendations, or of giving clearer instructions) in a short five-minute lesson to a small class, reviewing what happened with the aid of a tutor-observer and/or a video-tape record of the lesson, and then re-teaching the same lesson immediately to another but comparable group. It is one of the techniques which might contribute to the more analytic approach commended by Morrison and McIntyre and to the practice of self-observation which has been under discussion in this section.

Self-assessment is of persisting importance for all teachers who want to improve their competence, but, as suggested earlier, there are parts of the game that only an independent observer can see and it is time to look at the problems of assessment by tutors and regular teachers.

Assessment by tutors and teachers

It is so easy to dissect tutors' and teachers' assessments mercilessly. They do not always make clear what they purport to be assessing. They assess different things, and with varying relative emphasis, on different occasions and in differing circumstances. They use different terms to denote particular phenomena and operate from a wide range of fundamentally different value systems, both personal and pedagogic. They use different assessment scales and cannot be assumed to use any accepted scale with demonstrable consistency. They draw different practical conclusions from the same assessment evidence. They fail to encourage literally as distinct from relatively independent checks by assessors.

Anyone who finds such aggressive dissection too agreeable had better stop and think. Is it either feasible or desirable that there should be one unquestioned homogeneous set of criteria of teaching competence, and standardized means of applying the criteria? Values and circumstances vary in society. Teaching assessment is bound to vary with them. The practical problem is to identify what values are operating in particular circumstances and to reduce imperfections and inconsistencies in assessment that are due to operational faults. Such a fault might arise from feeble monitoring of what an assessment exercise actually does, so that avoidable inconsistencies or shifts of value are not made explicit with a view to future modification. In so far as more fundamental values enter the problem, each individual has, in any case, to use his own judgment and discretion. There is no mechanical way of eliminating fundamental differences. The art of living is partly the art of living with conflict.

Whatever the margins of error in assessing teaching, there is no doubt that there are some systematic differences in teaching competence. Until several years ago in one university education department graduates' teaching skill was summarized on what was virtually a nine-point scale from A+ to C−. In a year group of 138, one graduate had to do an extended teaching practice because of not reaching a minimal satisfactory level, while the others were distributed among the other grades as follows:

A+	A	A−	B+	B	B−	C+	C	C−
1	8	5	22	31	41	22	4	3

While it is doubtful whether one can discriminate accurately between immediately adjacent grades, differences become increasingly indisputable as one compares grades further apart. This can be partly illustrated by the following brief assessment notes, made at the time of the lessons, of a comparable set of students in another university.

1 A B+(?) lesson. The teacher read a poem to an able third-year class and discussed the poem with a view to getting the pupils to write their own poems in a similar style. He was fluent and articulate, used at least some names in addressing pupils, and had quite pleasant control of the class. However, there was too much time spent on exposition, and the exposition was over-intellectualized. One could imagine him getting better with experience. He was intelligent both in coping with his material and in subsequently defending what he had been doing.

2 A C− lesson. The first-year secondary pupils read out selected

short passages from the Bible. These were intended to illustrate different biblical modes—laws, history, poetry, etc. The pupils read aloud very ineffectively. It would have been better for the teacher to read aloud, or for the pupils to read silently and directedly. No pupil names were used. There was no building up of the intended product of the lesson on the chalkboard. The questions asked were extremely naïve. There was too much persistent chatter which mounted unchecked into complete loss of control before the end of the lesson.

3 An A— lesson. The young woman taking this lesson was concentrating on narrative exposition of the early explorations of Virginia. The pupils had their own maps and there was a map on the chalkboard. What made the lesson successful was the clear, bright, good-humoured, entertaining exposition and excellent rapport with the class springing from the teacher's lively and agreeable personality.

These lesson assessments were made in relation to three main areas:

Aim and structure. Clear aim? Right level of difficulty? Good timing? Some attempt to assess pupils' learning? Any kind of originality?

Teacher-pupil relationship. Reasonably good class control? Warmth? Reciprocation? Proportion of pupils involved? Pupils' enjoyment of the work?

Deployment of aids and resources. Questioning? Activity? Use of any audio-visual aids? Chalkboard? Voice? General deportment?

But, of course, one makes such assessments, still wondering how much depends on the teacher's personality regardless of the professional course, on favourable or unfavourable school atmosphere, on simply how well educated the teacher is, or on the chance factors that happen to operate within a particular class or even an individual lesson. This is sometimes reflected in conclusions such as 'C+ for actual performance, but B— if one makes special allowances for a slow class', or 'good plan but did not work with this class', or 'passable on this lesson, but one wonders what would happen in less easy circumstances'.

Some of the agony has been dispelled by the abandonment of fine grading. In the department from which the illustration of grade distribution was taken, not only has that grading system been dropped, but also a subsequent system with only three grades—fail, pass, and distinction (for, roughly speaking, the top 7–10 per cent). Reasons for abandoning 'distinctions' were that schools are felt to be more diverse now in the difficulty or ease of circumstances which may confront different students from the same year group, that teaching tasks (whether easy or difficult) have become more diverse, and that the term 'distinction' may suggest a kind of permanent pre-eminence when all that was intended was to distinguish those who were apparently pre-eminent in practice at the student-teacher stage.

One is left with the quip about when one intends to abolish the fail category. Provided that graduates who are least suitable for teaching withdraw as soon as they discover and verify their unsuitability (as some sensibly do), and provided that the others apply themselves really conscientiously, there is no absolute reason why all should not then pass. In practice there may be one or two in a hundred who either fail or require an extended period of supervised teaching, and several more who hardly deserve to be failed, although they strike one as weak teachers. People, including teachers, sometimes pretend to believe that more should be failed, but teachers and heads show themselves no readier than education tutors to bell these cats.

There is at least one reason for cautiousness. Teachers may do badly in one situation and surprisingly well in another, and vice versa. One has known a headmaster, supported by tutors, judge a student to be a definite failure. In less than a year another headmaster, having admitted the student to teach in his school in a special capacity, clamours for him to be re-examined and passed because he is proving so acceptable. Another student withdraws because he is quite sure that he has made a mistake in trying to train as a teacher, but within a short time decides that teaching does not revolt him as much as he thought. Another gains a teaching 'distinction' and then fares badly in a first appointment which proves uncongenial. Perhaps more should be failed, but one is assessing young people's career prospects at a critical stage and with many curious variables in the picture.

Neither is there reason for being unduly impressed by the known low correlation between tutors' and headmasters' assessments of student teachers and the assessment of the same teachers by other headmasters or experts after several years in teaching posts. The sources of such variation have already been discussed. Apart from the fact that teachers can change, at least to some extent, headmasters tend to give more prominence to characteristics that have to do with accommodation to the circumstances of particular schools, whereas assessments of student teachers are more influenced by general ideals of what a good teacher should be. Each assessment is perfectly reasonable within its own context. The differences are intelligible. One can live with them.

The practical requirements that face any tutor supervising teaching practice are (a) to help the student to develop his positive skills, (b) ultimately to recommend that he should or should not be recognized officially as having reached a minimal standard of practical competence, and (c) possibly to write a reference for him when he applies for a job. However positive and sympathetic and guidance-oriented a tutor may be, it is unrealistic to ignore that he has a responsibility to his own and society's standards as well as to the individual student. The student must share in this double responsibility. He has to use every help available for his own advantage, but he must also eventually supply the evidence that justifies recognition as a teacher and facilitates some kind of positive reference. It is interesting how even some mature teachers think of referees almost purely in terms of names to be put on a piece of paper, rather than in terms of evidence which might support the reference when it is written.

This discussion of assessment by tutors and teachers does not cover all of the problems nor all of the kinds of teaching that have to be assessed. For example, where (typically in some primary schools) pupil projects and group work are the order of the day, and where the regular teacher has a good system operating partly under its own steam, it may be difficult to assess what a student's contribution is, let alone how significant it is. One recalls the wry smile on the face of a senior Scottish supervisor many years ago as he commented, 'Of course, when I go to see that my primary students are doing the right thing I find the pupils doing everything. I can't see a student "teaching" '.

Despite the limits of this discussion, and particularly the use of examples which come conveniently from one's own recent experience, many of the points made are of general relevance. The flight from bad assessment threatens to become a flight from all assessment, but there were legitimate as well as questionable discriminations under older systems. It may be right to keep assessment firmly in its subordinate place, but its importance is inevitably reasserted when young teachers seek the material benefits of recognition and appointment. Employers and the public want to know what they are spending their money on. Also, there is a danger that assessment is driven underground if people go too far in underestimating the different quality of different teachers' contribution to their profession.

These last remarks are certainly not meant to reflect any complacency about the assessment procedures of teachers' employers themselves. They vary, but there are sufficient examples of inefficiency, ignorance, unfairness, and discourtesy to bring the correspondence columns of the teachers' journals to the boil from time to time. The young teacher must keep his own ear to the ground to increase his chances of a fair and courteous deal in the educational market-place.

The assessment of practical competence has been given priority, but the young teacher's knowledge of what is going on in the wider educational world is ultimately part of that competence—the political debates and manoeuvres, contemporary social trends, movements for innovation or counter-movements for economy, and the researches into major educational problems, whether their fruits are short-term or long-term. But some of these matters will be discussed later.

Assessment by researchers and theorists

What are the most practical points supported by empirical research into the assessment of teaching or by theoretical analysis of it? The answer is not any set of simple remedies or techniques. What we have now is a more subtle and detailed picture of the complexity of teaching. The picture was oversimplified in the past. Or, when its complexity was recognized, people tended to throw up their hands and conclude that, because much could not be analysed or controlled, therefore little or nothing could be.

The current practical interest in curriculum development, with its concern for defining objectives under the influence of theoretical educational taxonomies like that of Bloom (1956), reflects the greater analytic subtlety that is now available. Similarly, the refinement and caution that have entered processes of assessment, as illustrated in the preceding section, also represent a marriage of changing social attitudes and new analyses of assessment procedures.

While there is a persisting tendency for some extremists to over-react to the bad old days—partly, perhaps, because there are sufficient corners where the bad old days persist—there seems to be a growing awareness and exploitation of means of moderating some of the imperfections of assessment. Judgments are more cautious, more people are consulted, more different occasions of assessment are taken into account, particular kinds of assessment are viewed more coolly against wider perspectives.

Two researches that provide particularly interesting and clear examples of analytic research with potentially important practical implications are Duthie's *Primary School Survey, A Study of the Teacher's Day* (1970) and Hilsum and Cane's *The Teacher's Day* (1971). Dr Duthie was concerned with the highly practical problem of the possible employment of school auxiliaries to help primary school teachers with those duties which hardly require a teacher's professional skill. He concluded, on the basis of very detailed analysis of classroom activities in a representative sample of Scottish primary schools, that the allocation of one auxiliary to three teachers would economize valuably on teachers' time and effort. The kinds of activity to which auxiliaries might attend are extensively specified along with other practical suggestions about the proposal. On the theoretical side, the research is an important example of the application of the so-called OScAR technique (Observation Schedule and Record) of analysing classroom activities, as presented by Medley, Impelleteri and Smith (1966). This is a system of categorizing the main types of classroom activity and recording at frequent intervals which category applies in a given classroom situation. Also the researchers were feeling towards something less than a theory, but what they call a conceptual framework, for linking the psychology of learning with what happens in the classroom and with a taxonomy of educational objectives modified from that of Bloom (1956).

Bloom attempted to analyse the general patterns of all education so that these could be explicitly considered and used, no matter what the subject matter of any teaching might be. The six major categories are (1) knowledge, (2) comprehension, (3) application, (4) analysis, (5) synthesis, and (6) evaluation. Each category subdivides. Thus knowledge includes knowledge of specifics (e.g. that Dr Duthie carried out the research described above), of ways and means of dealing with specifics (e.g. the brief appraisal of what the research amounts to), and of universals and abstractions in the field (e.g. teaching compared with auxiliary duties, or the categories used in the OScAR system).

Similarly, analysis includes analysis of elements (e.g. the distinct activities observable in a classroom—kinds of question, answer, comment, etc.), analysis of relationships (e.g. the relationship claimed by some enquirers in this field between good learning and an encouraging, participatory atmosphere), and analysis of organizational principles (e.g. Dr Duthie's suggestion that certain activities invite organization on the basis of work by auxiliaries rather than teachers). Bloom's categories are not at all foolproof, and the companion study by Krathwohl (1964) on the emotional or affective domain has been dismissed by Richmond (1971) as 'doomed to failure and no mistake'. None the less, the volume on the cognitive domain remains suggestive for those who are trying to make their objectives less woolly.

The second research mentioned—by Hilsum and Cane (1971)—involved the study of 129 teachers in sixty-six Surrey junior schools in 1969. Means were devised of categorizing their activities during teaching hours, during intervals in the school day, and during their out-of-school hours. The report is full of vivid detail as well as statistical analysis. During teaching hours only about 43 per cent of the time was allocated to lesson instruction as such, 15 per cent to organizing pupils' work, 10 per cent to general supervision, and 10 per cent to clerical or mechanical tasks. During breaks and lunchtimes teachers spent only a quarter of the time on relaxation, eating, or private chat—the rest on miscellaneous professional activities. On average slightly more than two out-of-school hours a day were spent on professional work, and as much as 42 per cent of the teacher's whole work took place either during school breaks or out of school. These findings do not match some stereotypes of the teacher's life.

Both of the researches just mentioned are worth more detailed study, for they make very explicit some of the technical problems and ingenious solutions of this kind of study of classroom activities. It is not possible here to go into the details of the analytic categories used, but Flanders (1964), one of the pioneers of interaction analysis in the classroom, classified the teacher's talk according to whether it was talk (1) accepting the pupils' feelings, (2) giving praise, (3) accepting, clarifying, or using a pupil's ideas, (4) asking questions, (5) lecturing, or giving facts or opinions, (6) giving directions, or (7) giving criticism. Pupils' talk was classified according to whether it was (8) by way of response to the teacher, or (9) initiated by the pupil himself. And finally there was category (10) silence or confusion.

Apart from these categories of teaching or pupil talk, there were categories for other kinds of activity—(1) routine administration, (2) evaluation or correction, (3) periods of introducing new material, (4) teacher-pupil planning, (5) class discussions, and (6) pupils working at their desks or in groups.

Finally there were five scales of student attitudes—(1) liking the teacher, (2) finding school work interesting, (3) feeling that rewards and punishments were administered fairly, (4) feeling free to make some important decisions and to direct oneself at work, and (5) disabling anxiety manifested in certain paranoid reactions to the teacher's authority.

Flanders believed, on the basis of his research enquiries, that successful teachers, on top of their mastery of subject matter, tended to be better at

1 providing a range of roles, from the fairly active and dominant to the more reflective and supporting, achieving compliance but also encouraging pupil initiative;

2 assuming one role or another at will;

3 understanding the principles of teacher influence and translating these into appropriate courses of action; and

4 observing current conditions sensitively, objectively, and diagnostically.

The discussion thus far has been about certain attempts to identify more precisely what teachers do or might do. The ingenuity of such researches will attract those of an analytic disposition to study them more closely. But, even without closer study, it is obvious that important practical possibilities and considerations arise—particularly questions of the general economy of teaching, of what teachers should properly do and how they can best achieve their purposes.

The last main enquiry to be mentioned here by way of illustration is Rosenshine's survey of fifty-one studies of *Teaching Behaviours and Student Achievement* (1971). ('Student' means 'pupil' here.) These studies apply perhaps the severest assessment of all to the teacher's efforts. What demonstrable difference to measured scholastic achievement is associated with different kinds of teacher behaviour? For example, what difference is made by the teacher's expression of approval or disapproval? It seems that approval tends to improve achievement and disapproval to reduce it. The sceptics will hasten to deplore such a trivial confirmation of common sense. But there is a sting in the tail. The correlations tended to be statistically non-significant—that is, they might have been the products of chance.

What then about the teacher's 'cognitive behaviours' as they are called? Does the teacher's business-like orientation to achievement, his organizing skill, his clarity, his structuring of instruction, or the ease or difficulty of his lesson, influence pupil achievement? Here there is some reassurance, for the empirical enquiries mostly give a fairly positive indication. Other positive indications are for some association of pupil achievement with variety of environment and of cognitive mode, and with teacher enthusiasm.

The value of pupil-teacher interaction by means of talk—commended on certain grounds earlier in this book—does not apparently register itself in empirical studies of actual pupil achievement. Teachers' ratings of their own contribution correlate somewhat with pupil achievement, but achievement has not been shown in these studies to correlate with temporal factors, such as absences from school or other measures of time spent on a learning task. Teacher experience was positively correlated, but not with statistical significance. Teacher preparation gave mixed results, with some positive but statistically non-significant. Teacher attitudes even showed some negative correlations—perhaps a case of determined pupil response to pedagogic tartars? Teacher expectations correlated with achievement—but, asks Rosenshine, did the expectations *cause* the achievement (another matter) or simply illustrate the teacher's keen spotting of the most likely lads?

Rosenshine charts these fifty-one studies with admirable lucidity, system, and caution. Many researchers could benefit from his technical observations. For practical purposes one is left with reservations about the very mixed bag of researches (which Rosenshine fully recognizes), a readiness to be weakly consoled at those points where the empirical studies match one's preconceptions, a mild despondency on being reminded of the difficulty of demonstrating the causes of educational achievement, and a wariness about the larger claims of those educators who do not expose their confidence to the challenge of more analytic enquiry.

Retrospect on assessment

This chapter began deliberately with the problem of assessment as it impinges most directly on the student-teacher, went on to recall the wider function of assessment as a means of maintaining public standards and virtually helping people to trust one another at least a shade more than they otherwise might. It concluded with some illustrations of research work which has clear practical relevance, but which also goes beyond immediate practical questions alone—raising interesting questions of theoretical and technical analysis, which the beginning teacher can bypass, but which he might find interesting to examine more closely, and which may have repercussions on his eventual teaching career whatever choice he makes now.

Extreme opinions about assessment can perhaps be marginally justified as a means of sharpening the issues which have to be faced. However, the extremes seem very susceptible to demolition. The practical problems, the really difficult problems, are in the middle, where assessors of teaching are challenged to weigh up complex and subtle factors with technical efficiency and humane and balanced judgment. The technical efficiency can be acquired by application, and the judgment too—but over a much longer period of personal experience.

The student as teacher, 7
learner, and person

The student teacher does not suffer from lack of other people's high expectations on his behalf. He is expected to be a good student, a promising teacher and still his own personal self. He must sometimes be uncertain whether to feel more flattered or embarrassed by the high aspirations held before him. He may be comforted by those researches which have shown a tendency for the higher idealism of the training period to be supplanted by more down-to-earth attitudes on appointment to a regular job.

This tendency, of course, can be variously interpreted. There are times for idealism and times for doing what can be readily done in the circumstances. Some of the young teacher's capacity for becoming down-to-earth—that is, for acting expediently—may draw on skills developed during training. Some of the experienced teacher's later and more self-demanding reorientations draw, in turn, on the same idealism that is *one* proper part of initial training. Teaching has to be an alternation between feeling after more justifiable objectives and struggling with the practical pursuit of objectives that are currently accepted.

The preceding chapters have attempted to be practical in the sense of mapping out the factors that operate in the student teaching situation, suggesting various fairly structured courses of action which can be related immediately to actual teaching problems, and tempering all systematic advice with reminders of the teacher's inescapable responsibility to exercise his own discretion and judgment in the light of increasing experience. Giving priority to the immediately practical in these senses leads to simplification. Just as there is a certain alternation between defining objectives and trying to attain them, so there is an alternation between simplification for greater practical efficacy and periodic return to the actual complexity from which further simplifications may be wrested. It is rather like forming opinions about works of literature and art, only to be reminded by a fresh presentation of the originals how inadequate our opinions are.

This chapter is by no means intended to darken past counsel, but rather to extend and refine themes that have been partly adumbrated. In particular, it will discuss (1) some relatively new techniques of teacher training, such as microteaching and variants of the traditional school practice, (2) some aspects of the teacher's emotional and ideological position in relation to his work, (3) the double perspective that the student teacher has to have as a manager of his own as well as his pupils' learning, and (4) the question of whether there can be any general theory of teaching which might underpin the teacher's work in some fundamental way.

Microteaching

The last chapter referred to Dr Duthie's use of OScAR (observation schedule and record) in analysing what went on in Scottish primary school classrooms. More recently Stones and Morris (1972) have argued vigorously for a more analytic approach to teacher training, including the use of interaction analysis, microteaching, and analytic assessment scales, instead of the holistic, impressionistic, apprenticeship conception which they caricature as 'sitting with Nellie'. They claim that 'much of current practice is little better than a charade'. Their own proposals might be caricatured as 'sitting with OScAR'. The reasons for the proposals are a convenient introduction to the technique of microteaching.

Their argument is that the conservatism and other circumstantial limitations of schools and teacher-training institutions lead to unadventurousness and corresponding limitations in the practical initiation of student teachers. Students may simply have no opportunity to practise skills that are central to teaching. They may be more concerned with 'impression management'—that is with contriving favourable comments from teachers and tutors—than with evaluating what the pupils actually learn. They may be thrall to the regular teacher's superiority in expertise, power of criticism or commendation, and coercive power as an established member of staff. And, while the poor student is thus envisaged at the mercy of the regular teacher's appraisal, he is not, it is alleged, encouraged to make more extensive use of self-appraisal and, indeed, appraisal by the pupils.

If the proportion of traditional school practice were reduced and the proportion of microteaching increased, student teachers would be able to practise specified skills in simplified teaching situations, with the possibility of immediate appraisal of what could be improved and immediate actual practice in making the improvements. For example, a student might want to improve his skill (a) in asking more questions and (b) distributing his questions throughout the class. His micro-teaching practice might proceed in the following way.

1 Let us assume that a microclass of about six or eight pupils have seen or done a scientific experiment, or read a poem, or studied some other material that is a basis for discussion. If pupils are not available, fellow students can simulate at least some aspects of the pupil role.

2 The student takes his microclass for, let us say, five or ten minutes, during which he tries to elucidate the significance of what the class have experienced, and to ask as many, widely distributed questions as is reasonable and possible.

3 The student and/or the class members and/or the tutor comment briefly on how, if at all, the questioning could be improved. If the lesson had been video-taped it may be useful to pick out a small section of the lesson which vividly illustrates successful or improvable questioning technique. The emphasis is on this one skill and on what can be done immediately to improve a specific performance.

4 The student now takes over a different but comparable micro-class and teaches the same lesson, attempting to implement the points learned from the appraisal of the first trial.

Because of the nature of the skill in this example, one could have an almost numerical assessment. How many questions was each pupil asked? Or, did each pupil answer at least one question? Comment on the reasonableness of the questioning would, of course, invite more controversial discussion.

Two other examples can be taken from recent experiences with student microclasses. A mathematics graduate taught a brief intro-duction to set theory to a handful of modern language graduates. His objective was to get them to understand what a set was and what a Venn diagram was. The linguists and observers suggested some possible improvements and then the lesson was re-taught to a second group of linguists. In a kind of return match one of the linguists gave two mathematical microclasses a lesson in direct French. The objec-tive was to get the mathematicians to speak some French—which some surprised themselves by doing. Two points of minor interest about these cases were (1) that the introduction to set theory offered many possible treatments, so that there was perhaps too much room for dispute about what constituted a good introduction, while (2) the French lesson was so nearly impeccably done the first time that it was difficult to suggest improvements, although the student did correct a small point of usage on which he was mistaken.

Allen and Ryan (1969), in their clear and practical outline of microteaching in the United States, include in their examples of component teaching skills: (1) variation of stimulus to avoid boredom, (2) set induction, or orientation of pupils to the task to be undertaken, (3) reinforcement or encouragement of pupil participation, (4) posing of higher-order questions, as distinct from questions requiring simple factual response or recall, (5) use of illustrations and examples, and (6) planned repetition where this is a proper feature of a piece of instruction. They emphasize, as do others, the importance of working more or less on one skill at a time. Otherwise, one drifts back to the complexity of the ordinary classroom.

Buist (1972), describing the use of microteaching at Stirling University, refers to a scheme in which students practise eight teaching skills over a period of twelve weeks. Each microteaching session involves a twelve-minute lesson to a class of five pupils aged twelve to thirteen, followed by a review of the lesson (with videotape) and re-teaching of it to another class of five. Brown (1971), describing comparable work at the New University of Ulster, indicates how microteaching can begin with individual ten-minute lessons to five pupils and develop towards perhaps six interlinked twenty-five-minute lessons to ten pupils.

In both universities the microteaching is associated with instruction in the relevant aspects of psychological or pedagogical analysis, with a view to relating academic analysis more closely to teaching practice. Brown illustrates thus: 'in week 2 in psychology, the topic is the determinants of attention, in week 3 of the microteaching course the topic is gaining and holding attention.' And McAleese and Unwin (1971), also writing about Ulster, mention that one general goal of the students' twenty microteaching sessions is to sensitize them to the problems of real classrooms, so that 'during their third year full benefit can be attained from normal teaching practice'.

Student teachers are reported as liking microteaching. It has the advantage of concentrated and directed practice compared with the more diffuse and occasionally time-wasting character of some traditional school practice. The possibility of controlling the simplicity/complexity dimension, as well as lesson length and teaching objective, gives microteaching great flexibility and potential efficacy. It is a technique that stresses practice rather than exhortation, and that directs the mind to more effective practical analysis by providing relevant categories with which to do the analysis. It can exploit the self-revealing potential of the video-tape recorder, but still be used effectively even without such recording.

Allowing these attractive features of microteaching, one must add a number of qualifications. Enthusiasts are too ready to contrast the best features of microteaching with the worst of traditional school practice and pretend that this is a fair comparison. This does a disservice to both forms of professional preparation. Traditional assessment, for example, may have been based on more loosely analysed impressions—and some of the looseness, indeed, have been unnecessary—but impressions are not *merely* subjective and non-analytic. They vary from being mainly like that to being quite objective and analytic, even if the objectivity and analysis are not made explicit in a rating scale.

Similarly, one can have a teacher whose practical skill no one questions, but who does not think analytically about that skill. Even if an observer did the analysis for him, another teacher practising the analysed skills would not necessarily ever synthesize them into any performance comparable with that which wins the model teacher his reputation. The term 'born teacher' is sometimes used in an obscurantist, mystical way, but it typically denotes someone whose teaching skills are not entirely analysable and not readily matched by mechanical training alone. This is no argument for abandoning analysis or modelling, but for recognizing their limitations.

Another argument in extenuation of the shortcomings of traditional practice and assessment is that those involved in any enterprise are bound to have regard to the whole human evidence available. It is important to avoid unwarranted inequalities in training and assessment, but practical decisions and actions have to be taken constantly in the light of both public and private evidence. The typical human challenge is to do the best thing in highly particular and changing circumstances, not to limit one's actions to those which safely guarantee the highest possible consistency with other actions. Consistency is highly desirable but it is not a sole or completely overriding consideration.

The argument that traditional practice leaves the student too much at the mercy of regular teachers and leads the student into preoccupation with 'impression management' has enough plausibility to make it interesting, but it also tends to supplant reality with a rather cynical caricature. The managers of microteaching systems are bound to be in a very similar boat in respect of exercising power and inviting 'impression management', however much these realities are veiled with an objectivist apparatus of rating schedules and component skills.

Another limitation of microteaching is a defect of its virtues. It focuses attention on specific instructional practice. It is associated with attempts to formulate a general theory of instruction of teaching. This is a worthwhile line of enquiry for those concerned with teacher training, but it does not meet two of the typical shortcomings of professional preparation, namely, too limited experience of different schools and different sections of society, and too limited experience of the emotional and intellectual range of life outside the narrow scholastic rut. There is no reason why microteaching should be expected to deal with these problems—although it might, indeed, make a contribution—but they are problems that enter into the very practice of teaching, and it would be misleading to give the impression, however unintentionally, that the concept of teaching can be kept specifically instructional.

As so often in educational discussion, one really wants to apply different correctives to different viewpoints. The self-satisfied traditionalist wants a dose of microteaching and interaction analysis. The facile innovator wants to take a more sympathetic and accurate look at established practice. The way forward lies in combining the strengths and purging the weaknesses of different techniques.

Teaching practice variants

Apart from traditional school practice and microteaching there are other ways of practising teaching skills—some of them quite direct, others more indirect. Often these variants are, in a broad sense, striving in the same direction as microteaching—that is towards more specific purpose (although not necessarily the same purposes as those typical of microteaching), more limited objectives for any limited space of time, and more support for the individual student.

Study practice, for example, is the name given to systems in which a group of students visit a school, perhaps for a half-day each week, for a term or session. They may do some teaching and take part in other class or school activities, but they also make observations and use tests to build up an analytic picture of the psychological, social, and pedagogical factors relevant to the children they work with. Each student may concentrate his attention on a few of the children in a class and prepare a report of his observations and work over the period. Study practice, as its name suggests, attempts to link studies in education with the practice of education.

Another variant is to send more than one student to be responsible for a block of student-teacher work. It is a kind of embryonic team teaching. The students, in consultation with the regular teacher, plan a shared programme of work. Although team teaching is not very extensively used in this country, some student teachers may find themselves in schools where it is practised. This means that the regular teachers themselves operate a jointly planned programme, which allows different kinds of teaching in different sizes of group to take place according to what makes sense in the programme, instead of one teacher being constantly responsible for all of the work of one class of thirty to forty pupils. Team teaching generates what might be considered a new teaching skill—that of planning and implementing programmes within classes through detailed co-operation with other teachers. Teachers have always had to do this as between classes, but typically have been autonomous within the sanctuary of their own classroom.

Certain innovations that are not primarily related to student teaching practice at all may give the student almost a different kind of practice. Open plan classrooms are bound to influence students just as they are designed to influence pupils and regular teachers. Where a primary school programme is based on the 'integrated day' —a reaction against the disintegration of studies into periods of this, that and the other—the student is bound to get himself in some sense 'integrated' too. If a school uses 'family grouping'—as many schools in past times necessarily did—and brings children of different ages together in the same class, then the student must face a partly different set of problems. Even diversity of ability within a class of the same age presents different problems from a class that is homogeneous in ability. It may be, therefore, that special teaching practice experiences are a resultant of special features of schools, and not only of special theories about the best way of training teachers.

The teaching practice variants discussed so far have a plausibly direct connection with conventional assumptions about what schools do or should do. They are concerned with instructional objectives and with a certain understanding of the psychological and social backgrounds of pupils. The following statement by R. M. Jones (1972) reminds one of a possibly missing dimension—'Most teachers —I should say most teaching methods—place a tacit premium on remaining aloof from emotional references in subject matter not only when there is a good reason for doing so but also when there is not.' Is there a need for student teachers to do something about developing skill in understanding their own emotions and those of their pupils?

An associated theme is the importance of students and pupils doing their own learning rather than being manipulated into pseudo-learning by instructional techniques, however thorough. A *cri de coeur* from D. H. Hargreaves (1972) registers the point:

I have spent many hours preparing lessons and lectures. I have planned in detail the ground that must be covered, the content and structure of the lesson, and the nature of the fundamental concepts involved. But I have also had the disturbing experience of reading essays and examination papers of my own pupils

and students in which I could hardly credit the misunderstandings, distortions, omissions, irrelevancies and sheer
inventions based on the lessons and lectures I had so carefully
prepared . . . It is interesting that as soon as we become
teachers we completely forget what we felt and thought as
students.

Hargreaves then appears to swing from the extreme of instructional
idealism to an opposite extreme of Rogerian psychotherapy. Teachers
are envisaged accepting children unconditionally for what they are,
avoiding all attempts to evaluate their performance or to motivate
their behaviour by means of conditional approval.

The emphasis on the emotional and self-directing aspects of human
beings can generate quite different propositions, for example,

1 that the education of the emotions (in various senses which
require elucidation) should be a more prominent educational
objective;

2 that ordinary instruction would be more effective if teachers
paid more attention to the emotive aspects of instructional situations;

3 that learning would be better done if self-initiated in some sense
—even if part of the initiation is contrived by a teacher;

4 that learning should be mainly self-initiated or self-directed,
either on the liberal grounds that rational individual autonomy is
morally desirable, or on the radical Little-Red-Schoolbook grounds
that all susceptible youngsters should be encouraged to challenge
those in authority.

Since the student teacher is by definition both in and under teacher
authority, he is neatly or agonizingly placed to weigh up the issues,
but, as Hargreaves suggests, he may be tempted simply to detach his
two roles and avoid the complexities that seem to beset looking at
their emotional and self-directing aspects in one perspective.

It is not possible to discuss briefly the possible and desirable place
of emotion and autonomy in education, but one can mention
approaches to teaching practice that are based on giving them more
prominence both in the student's training and the teacher's teaching.
Some of the commonest are variants of a psychotherapeutic model of
learning. For example, the name t-group is given to a small group of
people who, with guidance, attempt to train themselves in understanding relationships with others by exploring their actual relationships over a period in a particular group. Instead of discussing a set
theme as one might in a traditional academic tutorial, or striving
towards some preconceived end as in microteaching, the group
member simply explores as freely as possible his feelings about the
others and their feelings about him and one another. There is a slight

analogy with one aspect of microteaching ideology—the idea of learning by doing, although t-group learning might be thought an attenuated form of doing, and, because of its elusive criteria of success, an attenuated form of learning. Elizabeth Richardson's *Group Study for Teachers* is a convenient and relevant illustration of a version of the approach.

Another practical approach to exploring the emotional along with the intellectual side of teaching is through role-playing. Again the idea is that one should not just talk about things but experience or practise them, even if only through a simulated enaction. It is hoped that exploration of simulated problems may sensitize those enacting the roles to wider aspects of the problem and possible ways of coping with it constructively.

Thus, one student might undertake to be a rather strict headmaster, a second to be his more tolerant deputy, and a third to be a student teacher who had persistently irritated the head by turning up late and by his very casual deportment and dress. The trio would enact a conceivable confrontation and try to resolve the problem. Or, in a second example, two students might enact pupils giving incompatible accounts of some school misdemeanour. A third would be the teacher questioning them to establish the likeliest truth and decide what action to take.

Such exercises can be devised to concentrate on the simulation of a relatively technical problem, such as examining pupils' conflicting stories, or practising diverse roles in order to get the feel of being in different persons' shoes. How might it feel to be an authoritarian head of department, or a lax but well-intentioned headmaster, or a student teacher suddenly asked to look after a class in a subject or age-range with which he was not familiar? How does one cope with a simulated 'disturber of the peace', or a 'quiet mouse', or a pretty but impertinent girl, or a loutish youth who happens to be a foot taller than you? As a simulated visiting tutor how would you discuss a lesson in which your simulated student teacher is imagined to have lost control of the class? These are random examples. The practicability of role-playing obviously depends on having students with enough relevant experience, problems that are sufficiently realistic, and a tutor who is sufficiently sympathetic to cope with what can be a sensitive exercise. One has heard of role-players coming to blows!

It is difficult to *prove* what is achieved by these techniques of emotional exploration, but some people seem to find them helpful, and they have a *prima facie* plausibility, at least as interesting possibilities for those who would like to try them out. Whether or not these are used, free discussion with intimate friends or with a genuinely sympathetic tutor remains perhaps the most important means of venting the student teacher's own anxieties and emotional problems. But temperament or circumstances sometimes block this outlet, which can only be unfortunate for both the student and his pupils. Carrying a load of personal worries is not the best preparation for freeing one's personality to share the emotional problems of pupils. The trite adage about a worry shared retains its force.

Single-minded enthusiasm is often necessary to push out the frontiers of exploration and invention. The microteaching enthusiast has to be swept away by the analysis of component skills, the psychotherapeutic enthusiast by the emotional depths beneath the tidy surfaces of human interaction, the sociological enthusiast by the social powers and ideologies that the educational system may too readily take for granted. For a person looking across the whole field of evidence there can be no justification for a monopolistic view of practical wisdom. Different approaches have different values. They are differentially relevant in different circumstances and for different people. They are resources to be used with discrimination in accordance with the purposes of particular individuals or groups.

Student teaching: the double orientation

As already suggested, the student teacher's double role does not necessarily pose any problem for him. Human beings are adept at switching roles, aided by many customary social and physical devices that help to define the areas in which particular roles can be readily enacted. Couples do not cuddle up in the back pew of the church as they do in the cinema. Children do not move quietly and warily in the playground as they do in the classroom. Students do not present themselves to their parents at home in exactly the same terms as to their fellow students in the union, or their tutors in the department. There might, therefore, be little relation between the student's experiencing of his own learning and his assumptions in organizing the learning of pupils.

If there is a closer relationship, what features of the student experience might influence student teaching at least marginally if not fundamentally? The general pattern of higher education is based on the assessment of written evidence that students know some of the main problems, techniques, and possible solutions within their field of study. The main instructional techniques include books, lectures, practical work of many kinds (essay writing, clinical experience, laboratory and field work etc.), and tutorial or seminar discussions. Serious study is such hard work and exposure to the guidance and assessment of specialists so demanding that some students have always kicked against the pricks of their academic bondage, even though, if they happen to be student teachers, they may still wonder why they cannot get all pupils to accept *their* bondage.

Student teachers are often made sharply aware of the great gap between the definition of studies derived from their student experience and the different definition which may be demanded by the limited horizons and capacities of many pupils. And yet one of the things that students persistently seek—more emphasis on discussion and understanding and less on factual memorization—is just what would be helpful to many of their pupils as well. There is no easy solution, for the underlying problem is a permanent tension that is bound to exist between exerting pressures to attain expedient objectives and sacrificing conceivable achievement to make the experience of learning more agreeable and possibly (not certainly) more illuminating.

The arguments are well balanced, wherever one's personal sympathies happen to lie. Instructional pressure can be painful and can lead to pseudo-learning that has no permanent consequence, but it can also help people to achieve more authentic learning and deeper understanding than they might originally expect. Freer, self-directed learning can degenerate into laxity and blindness to one's own low standards, but it can also produce a commitment and seriousness that are admirable. In practice, students are not sharply divided in these characteristics, but represent a wide range from the layabout to the pot-hunter, and from the person who seems to get a great deal out of his higher education to the person who takes his degrees and certificates while preserving a remarkable immunity to their intended educative effects.

Attempts have been made to measure the differential effects of different institutions on their students, but such large-scale research is difficult to finance, plan, and carry out with any hope of valid results. So many factors are at play that controversy tends to survive attempts to settle it. Common experience shows radical differences in the traditions, assumptions, objectives, personnel, resources, and relationships to society, that prevail even among different institutions of the same general type (e.g. universities), let alone among all institutions of higher education.

It might seem that such differences are bound to influence students. But can this be demonstrated, except in such matters as the kinds of job the products of different institutions tend to go to? Does the individual student retain the fundamental attitudes developed through early family life with little but superficial modification after the age of eighteen—or perhaps even after some earlier age? If the teacher is made, not born, is he made long before he thinks of becoming a teacher? But, even if there were positive answers to these wide questions (which is not certain), may not the modifications that can be made be of vital practical importance, because of the huge number of pupils who will benefit from even minor improvements in a teacher's techniques, attitudes, or understanding?

While some learning may be modelled by individual persons (the brilliant or dull teacher or lecturer), much learning is modelled by whole institutions or communities. The departmentalization of universities churns out its mini-specialists, who may pay only lip service to wider educational aims. The whole world of laboratory, clinic and hospital models life for the future doctor, just as a particular fragment of the school system does for the student teacher. Teacher education institutions probably vary more among themselves in ideological and technical emphasis than do medical schools, because of the different character of their studies. It may be that one important task is to extend each student teacher's school experience beyond the limitations of a particular locality, so that he is at least exposed to a wider range of models, whether or not he is influenced by them.

It might be expected that institutions educating teachers would be strikingly superior to other institutions of higher education in varied and effective use of appropriate teaching methods. Their lectures should not be too many, too dense, too rapid, too abstract, or too uniform for a diverse audience. Instead, they should be clear expositions of knowledge, expert introductions to the handling of evidence, striking dramatizations of significant situations, subtle evocations of mood, or ingenious stimulators of interest in important problems. (One has in mind some of the lecture criteria mentioned by Dr Ruth Beard (1970).) Their tutorials and seminars should not be private lectures, discussions of ill-prepared themes, or rambling coffee-table chats. Instead, they should contrive wide and informed participation, pointed discussion, discriminating and sympathetic appraisal, and openness to expression of the students' own problems and worries.

Their programmes should draw, where relevant and with adaptations, on those pedagogic principles that are thought appropriate to the school class—activities more varied than listening to lectures (which, of course, is also an activity—or should be), vivid exploitation of audio-visual aids, lucid chalkboard illustration, prompt and positive appraisal of student performance (or 'acceptance of student feeling' if that is the watchword), warmth of relationship in everything, and sympathetic insight into the student's psychological situation between adolescence and adulthood.

Of course, neither institutions nor individuals do reach such inhuman peaks of perfection—any more than a student teacher, assessing his own teaching, finds that it is absolutely faultless and unimprovable. In higher as in school education, people, circumstances and standards vary. Where teaching is generally good, teachers still may have unalterable idiosyncrasies—indeed, might be boringly uniform if they did not. And even a good teacher may have his occasional crisis of self-confidence when much effort seems to produce small effect, or the most earnest goodwill is deflated by an apathetic or cynical response.

In both school and higher education the inclination to revolt against the burden of exposition and examination is perennial. Centuries ago Scottish students, who were then more comparable in age and studies with today's secondary school pupils in an academic course, were protesting against dictated notes. And, in November 1963, the author was struck by a coincidence of theme between an essay which a graduate had just written on his own education and a report in *The Times* of a lecture by Professor Henry Chadwick, referring to Abelard, the early twelfth century philosopher and theologian. The student had written:

> Great as is the value of listening to a lecturer's words of wisdom, knowledge and insight of a far more lasting nature can be achieved from informal discussion and the comparing of different views (even wrong ones), and the very act of partici- pation ensures a deeper awareness of the problems involved in the quest for knowledge.

The report of Chadwick's lecture included these two sentences:

> Accordingly in the west, as Abelard showed in *Sic et Non* it was possible to recognize the absence of unanimity in the Fathers. Abelard presupposed that the task of higher education is not so much to pass on an authoritative corpus of securely established conclusions as to provide the student with the equipment to reach a responsible judgment.

Another vivid historical example of the perennial distress of trying to cope with studies that are at least temporarily beyond one's grasp can be taken from the autobiography of the late sixteenth century Scottish reformer, James Melvill. He went to St Andrews University in his early teens as was customary, but ran into difficulty with the Latin lectures of his regent (a Scottish forerunner of the professor). The following quotation is given in Scots to retain the period flavour.

> At the beginning, nather being weill groundet in grammer, nor com to yeirs of natural judgment and understanding, I was cast in sic a greiff and dispear, because I understood nocht

the regent's language in teatching, that I did nathing bot
bursted and grat at his lessones, and was of mynd to haiff
gon hame agean, war nocht the luiffing cear of that man
comforted me, and tuik me in his awin chalmer, causit me ly
with him selff, and everie night teatched me in privat, til I was
acquented with the mater.

Students today in their late teens or even older, as well as pupils in
schools, may still be cast into grief and despair even by lectures in
their own tongue, still brought to the verge of tears, and still have a
mind to go home again—and even do so. They still need the loving
care and comfort of someone (tutor, friend, or doctor) who will case
the strain of life and study when it becomes excessive. Whether the
strain can be minimized towards the point of elimination by the
kind of self-directed learning that Hargreaves commends or by the
methods associated with the name of A. S. Neill is a question of
wider controversy.

While the lecturing method has many charges to answer, these
charges are often more accurately levelled at excess to lectures or at
lectures badly prepared or given. There is still force in the remarks of
Paulsen (1906) that, in a lecture, 'a hundred little things, side remarks,
glosses, references to this and that, passing criticisms which one
cannot and is not willing to make in a book, are added, giving the
lecture the personal intimate character which no book can have.'
Moreover, the lecture is a valuable stimulus and discipline for the
lecturer as well as being a practical way of letting large numbers have
some direct experience of a scholar who can otherwise discuss his
ideas only with small numbers. The lecture 'constantly directs the
attention towards the *essential* and the *universal*' and exposes the
lecturer to the salutary 'opposition of the hearer who is repelled by
artificiality and sophistry'.

Paulsen may be too complacent for the more critical world of higher
education today, but he does remind one that there is something
to be said for a teaching method which is more often criticized than
favourably appraised. Bligh's *What's the Use of Lectures?* (1971)
gives a very systematic appraisal of the lecture, emphasizing its
value for communicating knowledge rather than stimulating thought
or changing attitudes, and suggesting many ways in which lectures
can be more effectively planned and supplemented.

There is no reason why the student teacher's double orientation
should be converted into a single orientation. There are obvious
differences between school and student life and between their respec-
tive aims, but the foregoing discussion at least suggests some points
where analogies may be drawn and where the student teacher may

find it interesting to compare his expectations of his teachers with his pupils' expectations of him. The discussion also provides a wider background to the question, now to be taken up, of whether there can be such a thing as a general theory of teaching.

Theory of teaching

Theory of teaching can mean a theory about objectives or a theory about ways and means. It is the latter that is intended in the present context. Bruner's theory, briefly outlined in chapter 5 in the discussion of programmes, envisages a system requiring the specification of (1) motivational experiences, (2) structurings of knowledge to facilitate simplicity and manipulability, (3) effective sequences of instruction, and (4) the nature and pacing of punishments and rewards. Microteaching, discussed earlier in this chapter, is similarly based on a theory of defining component skills of teaching, which, ideally, might be thought to make explicit all that (a) can be made explicit about teaching technique and (b) has any degree of generality to take it out of the class of hit-or-miss chance.

The Brunerian conception has been criticized by Jones (1972) for its incompleteness. It may be useful when the teaching is specifically instructional in character, but it overlooks the emotional aspect of education, which teachers too, in the routine patterns of school life, are already and perhaps unfortunately disposed to overlook. Teaching

> is a kind of work in which emotionally charged issues, appearing unpredictably as they usually do, are likely to be perceived as disruptive forces, alien to the purposes at hand, and therefore either to be avoided or met with a mind to dispelling them as quickly and summarily as possible.

Jones does not accept that 'if you concentrate on teaching children how to think, you will have taught them how to use their feelings appropriately'. There is a need to belong as well as to master, to play with possible concepts as well as form probable concepts, to transform as well as to absorb, to determine oneself as well as be determined from outside, simply to present oneself as well as to represent oneself in conventional categories. The first item in each contrasting pair may be more important to the practising teacher, even if the second items are more appealing to curriculum planners. The two sets are not mutually exclusive, but neither are they exactly the same things.

Just as there is a certain tension between the intellectual and the emotional as they struggle for a place in teaching theory, so there is a tension, mentioned earlier, between those who stress the centrality of persons in education and those who are drawn to systems or machines. Again there is no necessary mutual exclusivity, and neither brand of enthusiast would want to suggest that there was, but the 'persons' enthusiast is constantly threatened by lack of both specificity and generality, whereas the 'systems and machines' enthusiast is threatened by forgetfulness about both the vagaries of human beings and their necessary role in making even the most rational system of instruction genuinely significant and effective for those supposed to benefit from it.

'Theory' is one of the most elastic words, ranging in meaning from 'conjecture or opinion' to 'a coherent group of general propositions used as principles of explanation for a class of phenomena'. The extremes are not so dissimilar as might first appear, for both are concerned with imagining or fabricating general conceptions which help people to simplify and manage complex phenomena. The dissimilarity is in the objectivity and generality with which the simplifying exercise is carried out, and in the fruitfulness of the more sophisticated kind of theory in suggesting further hypotheses that are practically testable.

It is difficult to say precisely where theories of teaching stand by these criteria. Those with definite opinions perhaps tend to be at the optimistic or pessimistic extremes. On the optimistic side, writers like Bruner have at least focused attention on structural features of instruction which are logically and pedagogically plausible, and which are susceptible in principle of empirical testing. The possible over-emphasis on theories of learning is corrected by the reminder that instruction and learning are different kinds of thing. On the pessimistic side, some are bound to argue that *they* had not forgotten the importance of instructional principles, or that Bruner is just stating the obvious, without helping anyone to cope any better with the complexity of actual teaching situations, in which chance and improvisation seem so typical and inevitable.

This last line of thought is echoed, in the different context of the world of acting, by Dorothy Tutin's comments in an interview (*Sunday Times*, 7 May 1972): 'I think it's necessary to be surprised by life, it's so peculiar . . . A teacher can lend you attitudes and approaches, but there comes a time . . . when your performance is your own responsibility.' In the context of teaching itself it seems likely to be a continuingly open question how much derives from systematic theory of instruction, from attitudes and approaches, and from the responsible performance of the role one is challenged to accept.

Some may prefer, after all, to expect more help from a theory of learning than from a theory of instruction, but, as the author has argued in detail elsewhere (McFarland, 1971), the learning theory of psychologists offers the teacher very limited practical solace. The temptation is considerable for the practising teacher to react against rational analysis and go it alone with whatever makeshifts come to hand. Without denying the necessity of makeshifts, one does not see them as a foundation for any sense of professional teaching. Theory, on the other hand, can offer only a framework of thinking, not a detailed solution for every problem. The only professional path is a discriminating one between available theory and the limitations of actual circumstances. But theory may have to be a theory of educational objectives and methods, and not just of instructional techniques. The next chapter will take what can only be a first look at the link between the worlds of teaching practice and educational theory.

Teaching practice and educational theory 8

To put it starkly, the question of practice and theory is a question of whether teachers are to be considered intelligent and responsible adults, capable of defining and solving their own problems, or whether they are to be regarded as a kind of older child who can be given a limited measure of adult responsibility but is still to be firmly guided into channels mainly determined by others.

There are two escape routes from the more mature view of teacher responsibility. One is the route of imagining that one can do almost everything for oneself. Parents, theorists, administrators, critics—these must be kept off the scene so far as possible. The other is the route of imagining that one need do only what one is told, or what seems to be expected. This requires the art of shutting one's eyes to conflicting orders or expectations, and the studious avoidance of fundamental thinking. Some teachers make impressive attempts to escape down one or other of these routes, but the world outside school has such a nasty habit of coming into sight at every other corner.

Where one must sympathize with the practising teacher is in his constant exposure, not only to the brickbats of the workaday world but to the smart or authoritarian *pronunciamientos* of politicians, theologians, economists, moralists, and sociologists. A teacher-centred view of education (that is, treating teachers as well as children like human beings) must allow opportunity for blowing off steam in response to these irritations. In the longer run, however, teachers can only arm themselves with the weapons of the enemy. They must bring an adult intelligence to bear on the relevance of politics, philosophy and the social sciences, to educational practice.

The problems can only be broached in a chapter like this. What will be attempted is (1) to clarify some of the different things that people mean when they talk about theory and why some are fearful of theory, (2) to give some important examples of theories commonly

117

held by teachers, together with some comments on them, (3) to elucidate the power and limitations of the scientific model of knowledge, which in some ways obscures the necessity and importance of other modes of analysis, (4) to suggest the kinds of problem that require a philosophical rather than scientific approach, and (5) to discuss what the social sciences contribute to educational practice, and how far their contribution is mainly scientific or mainly ideological.

The meaning of theory

In the weak sense of theory ('conjecture or opinion') most people indulge at least occasionally in fragmentary theorizing. It is the stronger sense of the term that is of interest in a professional context —'a coherent group of general propositions used as principles of explanation for a class of phenomena'. The phrase 'used as principles of explanation' is significant. Theories are intellectual conveniences that justify themselves in so far as they help one to structure experience in useful ways. Theory, in its stronger sense, is used of structures that have at least some width of scope and that can stand up to more than the first puff of criticism. Colloquially, of course, people still say, 'My theory is . . . ' when all they are doing is expressing a passing opinion.

Since theories, even in the stronger sense, are still essentially matters of convenience, helping one to order and control the complex particularity of life, there is no reason why there should not be some conflict and disagreement even about quite well-conceived theories. This is not the same as saying, as some people do, that one theory is as good as another or that some decision *just* depends on what theory you *happen* to hold. The treacherous words are 'just' (suggesting falsely that one person's interpretation says all that can be said) and 'happen' (suggesting that a chance interpretation can be called a theory, regardless of its susceptibility to rational defence).

There are several senses of theory that are regularly confused even by people who purport to be educational specialists. One confusion is that already mentioned between opinion and theory. It is not that people do not understand the difference perfectly well, but that the latitude of ordinary discussion allows one to deploy words loosely and rhetorically in a potentially self-deceiving way. A second confusion is between hypothesis and theory. Here, too, it would be pedantic to insist on the verbal distinction, but it remains that there is a vital difference between a structure that has been plausibly envisaged (a hypothesis) and one that has been both conceived and in some measure tested (a theory).

The last important distinction is between a theory of how things happen and a theory of how they ought to happen. These are constantly confused in educational discussion, partly because of unclear thinking, but, to be fair, partly because teachers are challenged by practical problems which are partly problems of causation and technical control and partly problems of choosing among rival values. Thus, the theory of child-centred education sometimes means mainly a theory of how children can best learn, sometimes a theory that at least certain of the values of childhood should be preferred to the values of adulthood when children are being educated.

Theories of causation can be considered under two educational aspects. One may have a theory that social deprivation impedes school learning, which, if true, helps one to understand and tolerate certain kinds of slow learning in schools. Or one may have a theory that slow learners make the best scholastic progress if certain special facilities are systematically provided for them, which would be a theory of the causation of certain kinds of learning in certain circumstances—a kind of technical theory.

Confronted by any talk of theory, then, one could apply three tests to determine the kind of issue in question:

1 Is it a theory of causation, that is, either (a) a theory of the regular ways in which something happens or (b) a theory of the best way to make something happen?

2 Is it a theory of justification, that is, of what values, aims, or objectives *ought* to be preferred?

3 Is it a theory in the sense of (a) an opinion, (b) a systematic hypothesis, or (c) a theory in the fullest sense of a hypothesis that has stood up to at least some measure of rigorous testing?

The distinction between questions 1 and 2 is fundamental, but is regularly obscured by the rhetoric of language as people try to suggest that their personal evaluations or recommendations somehow have the force of fact. Here are some examples of suggesting that something is the case, while another word in the proposition indicates that a question of value is at issue:

There is a need for more nursery school education.
Child-centred education is best.
More use of educational technology is what we want.
It is worth considering where we would be without our academic traditions.

Any of these propositions can be defended or attacked, and factual evidence may be offered in doing so, but the propositions themselves are characteristically evaluative rather than factual.

The distinction between questions of cause and justification can, of course, be confused in more complex ways. As they become more complex, one is bound to suspect that someone is trying to pull the wool over our eyes. Consider this assertion:

But of course it's always easier for the authorities to carry on in the same old way.

Is this a plausible protest against inertia, or against authority? Is it really always easier in these innovative times to carry on in the same old way? What about the fact that different authorities act differently? Are all old ways bad? Will the recommended new ways automatically become bad in a few years because they will then necessarily have become old ways? Or is the assertion not meant to be a proposition at all, but just a protesting cliché?

Some theories and some criticisms

Since the theme is teaching practice and educational theory it may be useful to look briefly at some theories characteristically supported by practising teachers. The following small sample will provide an illustrative background to the relationship between theory and practice. In each case the theory is stated succinctly and then there is a comment (*) on salient features.

1 All children should be required to attend school between the ages of five and sixteen (or whatever other age range is specified).

* It has taken a century to act fully on this theory of the value of compulsory schooling. Many teachers have consistently supported the extension of schooling, but some have always questioned either the desirability or practicability of each extension of the period. The general theory is not unchallenged. Illich (1971), for example, without being completely convincing, has yet aimed some telling shots at the school as an institution for its costly instructional and educational failures, and for its alleged manipulation of prescriptive curricula and gradings in subservience to consumer-society values.

2 All children should receive religious education, or at least moral education, deriving at least in part from religious tradition.

* This very old theory of educational value is still widely supported today, although in a remarkable range of variants from hard-line denominationalism of conflicting kinds, through sundry *laissez-faire* attitudes, to atheistic moralism. Religion in education is still a theme that can bring blood to the boil and agitate politicians.

3 All children should be assessed in suitable ways in order to guide their subsequent careers and publicly certify their educational achievement.

* This could be considered a theory of value, like the previous two, or a theory of necessary means to motivating or guiding children towards recognized goals. Many would not give unqualified verbal assent to this theory, but fewer translate their dissent into even minor modifications of their own practice. It is, therefore, a prevalent and powerful theory, despite the cynical challenge expressed by such assertions as, 'Marks are used in school as a kind of bribe, to get you to do things you don't want to do'.

4 Teachers should have the right to discipline pupils by whatever physical, verbal, or social means are formally or informally accepted in a particular society.

* This theory of necessary means is very widely held. The nature of the aversive control varies among countries, but there are few stable learning situations where there is no such control, and there is some tendency for physical controls to persist either in principle or surreptitiously, even when their undesirability is avowed. When physical controls are genuinely absent, social controls tend to be emphatic, whether exercised through teachers, parents, or peers. This is equally clearly illustrated in communist and non-communist countries. And educational radicalism of the *Little Red Schoolbook* variety illustrates an attempt at aversive social control directed towards teachers instead of pupils. 'Grown-ups have a lot of power over you: they are real tigers. But in the long run they can never control you completely: they are paper tigers.'

5 The main emphasis of educational endeavour should be on helping children (i) to develop and use their present skills, attitudes, and knowledge, and hasten only slowly towards ultimate adult objectives, and (ii) to enjoy their present educational experience without feeling constrained by narrow prescriptions of expected scholastic achievement.

* This is a moderate statement of the theory of child-centredness. It can be thought of as a theory of objectives or of techniques. It has been most persistently cultivated in the context of primary rather than secondary education. Its specific interpretation is a matter of persistent controversy even in the primary school, and its slow progress in the secondary school is associated with inevitable differences in education as young people move towards the world of adult employment, and with necessary differences of interpretation springing from the distinctive psychological aspects of adolescence, as well as with the academic inertia of the secondary stage. Paradoxically, wealthier families in the West resemble communist states in subordinating child-centredness to more general public and social ends, although with different kinds of public end in mind.

6 Children should be enabled to acquire the knowledge, skills, and

attitudes that educational tradition and innovation can offer them.

* This tends to include, more or less universally, the skills of reading, writing, counting, and behaving morally—however varied the detailed interpretation of these. There is also a fairly general tendency for the specification to go on to include, in some form, history, geography, mathematics, science, foreign languages, music, art and craft, religious education, and physical education, although obviously, with still greater variations of interpretation. This is a theory of the value of the community's developing cultural heritage and also of the necessary means to earning a later living in the community. It is another case where the sorting out of ends and instrumentalities is necessarily complex, but the relative (some say excessive) stability of educational systems betokens considerable effective if not principled subscription to the theory.

Again Illich (1971) is one of the most rhetorically, if not logically, cogent challengers of the theory, on the grounds that a society corrupted by a minority's extravagant consumption is not fit to prescribe an irrelevant cultural diet for the masses. He imagines a situation in which people would acquire what skills they wanted when they wanted them, and educate themselves by a system of easier *ad hoc* access to educative things and people. This seems to be a Utopian extreme of individualism, contrasted with communist radicalism, which employs traditional scholastic values and techniques, but for the purpose of upholding its own kind of state.

The theories just listed are quite broad, quite substantial in significance, quite widely held by practising teachers, and quite far-reaching in the detailed educational practices they are held to justify. They are elaborated with considerable detail and clarity both in writings about education and in institutional practice, which is virtually an alternative statement of theory, a working model. Radical theories by definition cannot be widely, or even at all, represented in working institutions. Radicalism constantly destroys itself, whether by success or failure. Nevertheless, radical theories are also clearly elucidated in writing, and successful radicalism demonstrates the readiness of societies to respond, sooner or later, to criticism if it is intrinsically cogent.

It seems, therefore, that educational theory does what one expects of theories. It provides general principles of understanding to guide perception and action, and it provides a means of criticizing and transforming fundamental assumptions and practices. Children are sent to school, which, *pace* Ivan Illich, is better than putting them down mines nineteenth-century-fashion, or even into some of the typical employments that might use them today. Moral education is more humane (or, some may prefer to say, more genuinely religious).

The curriculum is more varied. The sensitivity to unequal opportunity is greater. The specialized means of assessing and supplying the varied range of educational needs are more highly articulated both in intellectual analysis and in educational practice. Subtler interpretations of values and techniques do stimulate and sustain better practical education, even if it takes small acquaintance with the practical world to appreciate that not everything changes for the better and not all problems are solved.

The fear of theory

Despite the clear place of theory in relation to any set of educational practices which are to be considered justifiable and not just expedient, the idea of theory obviously perturbs many teachers, both beginners and the more experienced. The James Report on *Teacher Education and Training* (Department of Education and Science, 1972), referring to the initial professional training of teachers, says with phobic caution, 'It is not suggested that educational studies—that is, history, philosophy, psychology and sociology of education—should be banished . . . but only that their role should be seen as contributory to effective teaching.' But one of the points of studying education is to examine critically the meaning of 'effective teaching'. Even the consensus of practice is imperfect, and the consensus about rational aims and methods is always under dispute and often the subject of radical challenge.

Kemble (1971), in a different kind of book about teachers, expresses the Jamesian attitude in these terms: 'Any discussion of the question, What makes a good teacher? must be related to the coal-face reality of the classroom.' One of his fellow contributors tells us that 'real people, not statistics and classifications, are the subject-matter of education' and that 'there needs to be a knowledge gained from contact with real people in real situations'. And another was aware of the gap between the science he was teaching and the needs of industry, which 'reflected the way in which schools are cut off from the real world'.

These examples are typical of a quite common urge to give special, although not necessarily clearly specified, status to a particular situation or person, and to withdraw status from some other situation or person which is supposed to possess it currently. The school classroom is to be considered more real than, let us say, the student seminar on school classrooms. But the school in turn and its teachers, including presumably its student teachers, are to be considered less real than the world outside school. Or, in a common form of the cliché, their reality is less real because it is middle-class instead of working-class reality, with the paradoxical corollary that our society is both too class-conscious and not class-conscious enough.

At this point in the pursuit of ultimate reality another paradox supervenes. A benevolent intention has run into a logical muddle and one has to go back to the 'unreality' of the philosopher's study to unravel the phoney categories that are employed by the same radical breath that condemns them. The literal question underlying the muddle is about the proportions of different kinds of study and activity that student teachers or school pupils should be offered, about the balance between induction to present assumptions and circumstances and induction to techniques of criticizing these assumptions. It seems that some young writers might concentrate on inducting teachers into relative acceptance of pupils as they are, but pupils into relative rejection of schools as they are! Whether this would lead to what has been called 'constructive tensions' is perhaps debatable.

There are some obvious practical reasons for the anxiety occasioned by the idea of theory in the minds of many practitioners. There is the legitimate distaste for having someone else suggest either that one should be aiming at something different or using different techniques, especially as only the person on the job knows intimately the detailed circumstances and resources with which he has to work. The danger, of course, is that actual circumstances and resources may fetter one's imagination completely, but an able practitioner would be able to demonstrate where he was defying circumstances as well as where he honestly believed they had to be at least provisionally accepted.

A second practical reason is that educational problems are so complex in terms of unravelling causes and elaborating cogent justifications that even people one might call professional theorists tend to be subdivided by separate specialisms, each with its enormous literature. Why should the classroom practitioner not preserve his specialist authority in the practical field? A third reason complements the second. While only a few have enough time and inclination to struggle with the increasingly technical demands of education as an area of scholarly or scientific study, many more are called upon to expatiate upon education in relatively popular contexts where entertaining rhetoric or political persuasiveness may cut more ice than refinement of academic analysis.

In the case of student teachers many would share the Jamesian view that plenty of practice and very little theory constitute the right formula. Theory is liable to direct one's attention to factors that are beyond one's control, or that may influence other people's corner of the world but not one's own; or, if they do affect one's own teaching practice, it is too perplexing to think about them anyway. Is it not enough to cope with things as they are?

While sympathizing with the sentiment, one cannot support the general viewpoint. There are many situations, both for student and mature teachers, in which just coping is a satisfactory or even impressive achievement, but it is not an acceptable general standard of professional competence. Few teachers would accept such a minimal standard for themselves, even if the public were prepared to accept it. Nor does plenty of practice meet the bill. Plenty of practice can be extremely bad—when it is practising either the wrong thing (which it sometimes is), or a very restricted or untypical range of things (which it quite often is). Even plenty of good practice sacrifices an extra dimension of its own value if it cannot stand up to both positive analysis of its virtue and reasonable criticism of any shortcomings from what is desirable and possible.

This analysis of the fear of theory suggests, therefore, that theory and practice are in the long run inseparable. There are occasions when teachers are right to challenge theoretical pronouncements and when theorizers (including teachers) are right to challenge accepted practices. Theory can be unrealistic fantasy, but also imaginative innovation. Practice can be dead and ineffectual convention (an easy mark for Illich), but it can also give the lead to fresh theoretical analysis and desirable policy change. That tension will persist is inevitable. One has to hope that it will be the 'constructive tension' mentioned two paragraphs ago. In the meantime, there is still the more specific question of what practice can expect from the various separate disciplines of education that are commonly summed up in the shorthand 'theory'?

The study of education

A digression on science will help to clarify the study of education, for the study of science has been the dominant model of worthwhile and effective study for the past century or thereabouts. It took science several centuries to reach this position, for it had to compete with the rival literary and philosophical tradition of classical culture, which had the advantage of a couple of millennia rather than a mere two or three centuries behind it. Today science, while striving to keep its academic shrines pure, is sustained materially by a vast power of either destroying life or prolonging it and improving its physical comfort.

The intellectual and material power of the scientific model of study is important, for it has made many people less able to understand and accept that there are many kinds of problem—moral, historical, aesthetic, for example—which cannot be solved by science. It is not that science happens not to have reached these problems, but that science never could reach them. Science can contribute to their discussion in an ancillary and technical manner, suggesting or confirming the physical possibilities of situations—dating archaeological specimens, analysing pigments, specifying the properties of medical drugs. It cannot, and is not required to, supply moral, historical, or aesthetic answers by mysteriously transcending the intrinsic characteristics of these fields, namely, their subtle intermixture of objective evidence and subjective interpretation. Such fields are not fields where scientific experimentation is imperfect, but where it is mainly irrelevant for the central task.

Science is, of course, a consideration in such contexts, but as an incidental circumstance, not as a fundamental means of resolving problems. Science gives rise to moral, historical, and aesthetic problems, but it cannot solve them experimentally. If one puts aside the distinctive feature of science—its experimental testing of precisely formulated hypotheses—scientists still share with other kinds of specialist a common respect for objectivity, logic, and precision. Potentially, these shared criteria, can be brought to bear on any kind of problem, but, in fact, individuals vary greatly in capacity to transfer their intellectual virtues beyond the sphere of their specialist training. Many trained in science are put off if they have to face problems that are not susceptible of laboratory constrictions and control, just as many trained in the arts will run a mile rather than do an elementary sum.

This leads to the question of how scientific study has influenced the study of education. Since one whole area of educational theory has to do with philosophical problems, particularly problems of ethics and the nature of knowledge, and since these are intrinsically difficult and debatable (but not merely subjective), two kinds of student are liable to have difficulty. At one extreme there is the rigid experimentalist or mathematician who has little time for problems that cannot be answered conclusively, despite the inconclusiveness of science itself at its growing points. At the other extreme there is the woollier kind of arts man who slides away from precision and objectivity even where they are easily attainable in his own sphere.

While certain incapacities are apt to be associated with particular disciplines, it is those who have either a narrow or a feeble conception of their own discipline (whatever it is) who perhaps tend to be least able to confront the challenge of philosophical problems, which, none the less, remain inescapably there in the countless value judgements that teachers make from day to day in their classrooms.

Apart from the inescapability of moral problems in particular, philosophy is relevant to sharpening the teacher's power of analysing the many common illogicalities of educational (and other) discussion:

1 Unwarranted generalization, arising from the temptation to distract attention from the circumstantial limitations of one's experience, observations, or experiments.

2 Contrasting the best of what one favours with the worst of what one opposes, instead of like with like.

3 The genetic fallacy of imagining that an argument is *necessarily* invalidated by giving an account of its motivational origins (e.g. that loathing a particular individual *necessarily* invalidates one's criticisms of him).

4 Confusing logical categories, e.g.:
   (a) One may treat 'There is a need for . . .' as if it were a simple statement of fact rather than a conditional statement (a need for water—*if*, literally or metaphorically, one is dying of thirst; a need for more schooling—*if* more schooling will achieve what is desired).
   (b) One may treat a concept like 'mind' or 'intelligence' as if it were some unitary thing—Gilbert Ryle's famous 'ghost in the machine'—whereas, whatever one's detailed analysis, these words refer to very complex relational phenomena which are difficult to analyse.
   (c) One may confuse, as people frequently do, two concepts like 'social' and 'sociological', treating them synonymously, whereas the first means 'pertaining to life and relationships in a community' and the second 'pertaining to theoretical analyses of life and relationship in communities'. There is a similar problem of 'history', which refers both to 'what has happened' and 'what historians make of what has happened'; or of 'education', which refers both to 'the process of contriving people's self-betterment' and 'the study of the process of contriving people's self-betterment'.
   (d) One may treat a question of values as if it were a question of fact, as where change is made synonymous with progress. Any difference makes a change. Only a difference in a favoured direction can qualify to be called progress.

5 Failing to identify the rhetorical character of utterances, and to distinguish literal meaning, emotional tone, the speaker's intention, and the actual effect on listener's thoughts or behaviour. Thus, the statement, 'You do have a super dress on today' has a fairly clear literal meaning. One knows the words and the syntax. But, while the speaker might intend to ingratiate himself, his tone might be too emotionally emphatic, and his effect might be to evoke a reserved response. To take an educational example, a teacher might give a clear analysis of the educational situation, his intention might be to gain a reputation for powerful and intelligent comment, his tone

might be warm and trenchant, and his effect might be to divide the audience into admirers and detesters.

These are important, although not entirely systematic, examples of how the logical aspect of philosophical study (one does not mean necessarily logic as a systematic academic study) can strengthen teachers against the seas of rhetoric and loose logic that inevitably wash through the social and political, and not just the educational, scene. Rhetoric here is used in its widest sense—every aspect of symbolic utterance that gives the utterance its characteristic tone, whether it is the scrupulousness of a scientific paper (concealing its always messier genesis), the reverberant articulation of scientific, historical, or literary abstractions (giving high and serious tone to the discipline), or the runaway gift of the gab that makes a popular orator more plausible to hear than to think about.

Where philosophy can be frustrating to the practising teacher is in its tendency to corrode conventional assumptions without replacing them with anything positive, and in its tendency to take on the character of a refined intellectual game, like chess, while teachers and other practitioners struggle with substantial problems that are not at all play-like. The philosopher's academic subtleties become autonomous—studiously, even pompously, detached both from empirical science and everyday practical problems. Philosophy is a purely critical discipline, chilling to those who are trying to get something done in ordinary life. It drives one to a cold-baths-are-good-for-you kind of defence. Even other traditional academic disciplines, like history, literature, or science, are wary of philosophy because of its undermining tendencies. Despite these difficulties, it is just this fundamental character of philosophical analysis that makes it one of the most important techniques of clarifying educational and other concepts. It influences educational practice by changing educational preconceptions—at any rate, in the long run.

Apart from philosophy, the social sciences are the other main disciplines contributing to educational practice. In particular, psychology has attempted to create a scientific framework for analysing human behaviour, while sociology has tried to do the same for human institutions (families, schools, churches, bureaucracies, social classes, etc.). The author has discussed some of the main problems elsewhere (*Human Learning* (1969) and *Psychological Theory and Educational Practice* (1971)). It would be inappropriate to go into the details in the present context. What is relevant to the present discussion is to identify the general character of the social science contribution to education and some of the problems that it poses for practising teachers.

One of the superficial problems is the huge range of sophistication about such matters among different groups of teachers—from those who have imprecise ideas about what psychology and sociology are, or are trying to do, to those who think that most practical educational problems are just waiting the magic touch of behavioural or sociological programming. Social scientists themselves are divided in their allegiances to empirical measurement, theory-building and practical policy-making. One group is for giving people tests or systematically interviewing them. The second is for devising speculative structures which, hopefully, may eventually be tested against empirical evidence. The third is impatient for action, almost like the anti-theoretical kind of class teacher.

When even physical scientists feel threatened by the moral problems posed by the technical applications of science, it is not surprising that social scientists, whose very subject matter is the human world, should find it difficult to be completely loyal to their scientism when confronted by the possible moral enormity of their data. They are caught between the pulls of science and ethics, without usually being as scientific as the physical scientists or as philosophic as the philosophers. It is not surprising that some should be drawn into the limbo of ideology, where science, philosophy and dogma can be mixed according to taste.

One of the sharpest lines of attack on the social sciences is not that they are imperfectly scientific in technique or achievement, although that is manifestly the case, but that their central problems are intrinsically incapable of solution by scientific analysis alone. The attack is made with unsparing trenchancy by Louch (1966). More recently, Hudson (1972), in his autobiographical *The Cult of the Fact*, has probed into the soft spots of psychological scientism and advocated, probably with little chance of convincing academic psychologists, that psychological research should have practical human relevance as well as scientific respectability. He seems to echo a long-standing cry from the school classroom.

The hard core of the philosophic challenge to the social sciences is that one cannot explain human behaviour without reference to human values and purposes (objectified in the social and cultural world), and to the creative character of much human action. Neither psychological nor sociological categories can in any sense reduce the particularity and originality of behaviour and experience. They can only group past behaviours and experiences in ways that may have a simplifying utility. But psychology and sociology become history even as they are written, or else they become ideology. Exactly repeatable experiments are apt to be few and sometimes trivial. Hypotheses or theories and the evidence for them are at best loosely, even if interestingly, related—much as with educational theories.

The history of psychometrics, or mental measurement, provides a good illustration of how psychology and sociology run on to controversial ground even as they use their own concepts, such as the concept of measured intelligence or membership of a social class. These concepts are so wide and variable in interpretation that disputes about empirical findings readily turn into disputes about how phenomena should be valued—one skin colour or cultural tradition compared with another, verbal compared with manual skills, co-operative compared with either competitive or rebellious attitudes. But the social sciences, like philosophy, continue with their undercutting exercise, disturbing what may have seemed firm ground and striving to establish their own new basis for thought and action. Like philosophy, therefore, they are simultaneously stimulating because of the fresh concepts and evidence they present and alarming for those who are not accustomed to defending their own values from intellectual attack.

It is impossible to strike any exact balance between the benefit and the harm that the social sciences have done to the practising teacher. Some of the harm is associated with the tendency of educators themselves to grab at any author or theme that can be plausibly related to educational practice. This concern for practicality can be self-defeating when the social sciences or philosophy are used like one of those advertisements that give the supposedly hard scientific reasons for buying a product which is going to be put on the market in any case. One sometimes feels that a new season will bring a different advertising campaign but virtually the same educational product.

The social sciences and philosophy perhaps lack a sufficient sense of their fault-finding image, or, if they have such a sense, are too proud of it. Philosophy can at least say that it no longer presumes to tell people what to do, and, as we have seen, is criticized for this reticence. The social sciences are very inclined to tell people what to do—no matter what subtleties of scientism may be used to clothe their intent. Perhaps it is best when the intent is to advocate quite specific social policies. Then one can at least assess specific cases—some of which may be very strong.

But often the social scientist sows a sense of unease without clarifying a problem constructively. He makes his fame with subtle analyses of teacher role, but leaves the teacher more doubtful than ever about how to view himself and his job. He devastates conventional assessment systems with his statistical comparisons and analyses, but ignores the wider contexts of assessment, and almost certainly exemplifies, in some aspect of his own practical or professional life, the very assessment vices he attacks. He ingeniously unearths cultural bias in educational systems but leaves a sense that teachers are just an incidental parameter in his sociological model. He would transform education but not himself teach—at any rate, not children.

It remains, when all these criticisms are made, that psychology and sociology have sharpened teachers' thinking about various things relating to educational practice—the apparent, even if partly disputed, psychological needs of children at different stages and with different learning difficulties, the pervasive influence of spoken language in stimulating or limiting children's educational development, the power of family encouragement or apathy over educational achievement, the subtle assumptions about different classes of children that get firmly rooted in teachers' minds, the significance of a predominant orientation to scholastic or academic achievement in a community where most people (perhaps even most academic people) are mainly concerned with other kinds of achievement, or the possibility of improving the unavoidable business of human assessment by technical means and also by wider perspectives on the whole problem.

It is important to recognize the intrinsically intermediate character of the social sciences, standing between the ideals of scientific objectivity and social justice. But this does not mean that they *never* succeed in attaining to either of the ideals. The attempt to be objective and just has been greatly aided, as well as occasionally confounded, by the work of social scientists. It makes sense for teachers to penetrate some potentially relevant sector of the social sciences in depth rather than to fall for the eye-level appeal of the first package that looks as if it might sweeten some educational pill.

The contribution of the social sciences to education has probably been mainly ideological—not in any derogatory sense of the term, but in the sense of tending to shift people's perspectives by a combination of hard evidence, systematic speculation, and appeals to a common sense of justice. Since there is bound to be conflict at all three levels, one simply has to accept the intrinsic contentiousness of the material and try to pick one's way through it with cool discrimination. The fact that nobody can escape entirely from his personal psychological or social framework is not an excuse for abandoning the standards of rationality and objectivity. They are the only means of progressing beyond purely emotive confrontation, and there is plenty of evidence that they sometimes work successfully, even if there is also plenty of evidence of their failures.

Perspective on practice and theory

Student teachers vary greatly in their interest in educational theory. This is obscured by general and sometimes prejudiced opinion polls, which understandably show that in a simplified choice between theory and practice students will tend to emphasize practice. Students who would happily drop educational theory in the rubbish bin are matched by others who have a very deep concern about the wider issues of their work in education and society.

The limitations and frustrations of theory have been thoroughly examined and there is no need to stress them further. Recognizing them is the easy part of the exercise. The difficult part is for teachers to find their way through the constantly expanding fields of the social sciences and the constantly more refined processes of philosophical analysis. Since these tasks are intrinsically complex even for specialists there is no hope of their being easy for anyone else. The student teacher is necessarily dependent on the intellectual and pedagogic sophistication of his instructors or tutors.

What is wanted must vary with time, place, and persons. Social and psychological subtleties will be there on the very first teaching practice, but a student teacher is not likely to be concentrating on them. A mature teacher may be very ready to discuss the subtleties of teaching situations. There is a time for assiduous study of facts (despite the popular tendency to discountenance factual study, contrasting it falsely with 'intelligent understanding' or some such phrase), but also a time for reflection, analysis, and speculation. Much futile dispute about theory is really a dispute about best times and occasions for doing various things.

The simple plea for theory that is clearly relevant to practice is understandable but not entirely acceptable, for it mistakes the kind of contribution that theory can make to practice. Theory does not typically give one specific instruments for practical purposes. Physics and mathematics do not build bridges, but an engineer who was ignorant of these disciplines is not a person with whom one would place a contract. One would still not place the contract if the ignorant engineer promised to learn as much mathematics as was necessary as he went along. One wants more assured resources. And this is true of teaching as well.

To imagine that the study of theory can supply uncontroversial and speedy practical solutions is to mistake its nature and to overlook the detailed arguments outlined earlier in the chapter. But neither can practice alone supply such solutions. Many stubborn teaching problems resist years of practice, and many of the solutions observed in practice are controversial indeed. It is difficult to see any intelligent and practical solution other than exploiting both intelligence and practice, systematic study and systematic experience.

Every effort should certainly be made to give priority to those areas where theory and practice come most closely together—for example the significance of developmental stages, social influences on school education, and the relationship of ethical analysis to the moral problems that face young people. But this utilitarian approach should allow for some fundamental study of concepts and evidence, however selective, if it is not to become a mere ornamental top dressing. The most fruitful eventual interaction of theory and practice depends on periods of separate attention to each, as well as on other periods when their more direct mutual impacts can be explored.

Appendix A

Student teacher's check list

The list is formulated as a planning list, but, with some changes of tense, it can be used to diagnose necessary improvements over past performance.

A   Objectives

1 What are (a) the characteristics, (b) the requirements, (c) the opportunities of this teaching situation?
2 Are there any ways in which I could be more courteous or helpful to pupils or staff?
3 For each unit or section of teaching:
   (a) What are my specific and manageable objectives?
   (b) What are my genuine resources?
   (c) What is the detailed programme of work for the pupils and for myself?
   (d) Is the work easy/hard enough for these pupils?
   (e) What have I done to allow for the range of abilities among groups or individuals if this is wide?
4 At any given time, what pedagogic skills am I concentrating on improving?
   (a) Formulating objectives?
   (b) Improving control of learning processes and of good behaviour?
   (c) Improving mastery of my subject skills in relation to these pupils?
   (d) Observing and assessing the pupils' learning or conduct?
   (e) Organizing resources and programmes for learning?

B   Control

In addition to the checks under **Objectives**, which are relevant to control as well,

5 How much of the available time have I allotted to guided activities by the pupils (including answering questions)?

6 What provision have I made for
   (a) variety of activity during longer periods?
   (b) choice within activities, if relevant?
   (c) making clear the point of major units of work?

7 What will I do to ensure that the pupils experience enough successful achievement to motivate further learning?

8 What will I take care to commend and to discourage, and what kinds of comment will I use to achieve firm but friendly guidance?

9 In what ways may I be able to model the learning I want achieved (e.g. clarity as an aid to clarity)?

10 How will the pupils' work be assessed (e.g. by comment, completion of task, questioning, etc.) and how will I ensure that any process of incidental assessment does not interfere with the work of the class (e.g. undue concentration on one person or group)?

11 How will I contrive to use pupils' names as freely as is feasible, and to strike a friendly but not over-permissive note?

12 What kind of misbehaviour will I take care to reprove promptly, quietly, and firmly? And in what terms will I try to redirect the attention of misbehaving pupils to more co-operative and constructive tasks?

13 How will I show from time to time that I am not interested in the pupils just as recipients of my lessons?

14 Have I consulted the regular teacher about any more serious problem that has arisen or that I fear may arise?

C   Subject Skills

15 Am I exploiting what I really know and am interested in, or am I using too much hastily collected deadwood?

16 Am I keeping my subject skills alive in an adult way for future as well as immediate teaching purposes?

17 How can I transmute an adult vision of any topic for the benefit of pupils without dimming it?

D   Observing and Assessing

18 How will I ensure that all individuals or groups in the class get a fair share of attention and assessment at one time or another?

19 How will I ensure that pupils continue with their various tasks even when they cannot have much attention for a period of time?

20 How will I assess how far the class as a whole is learning what it is supposed to learn?

E Organization

21 In what units will the class operate (as a whole, as individuals, in sub-groups)?
22 How will necessary resources be mustered and deployed?
23 What is the time-table intended for the subsections of any programme?
24 What interruptions are possible and what strategies are available to modify the intended plan of work?

Appendix B

Teaching method: some illustrative readings

Whether or not subjects are 'integrated' in teaching practice, a major part of teaching skill has to do with understanding particular subjects and how they can be used in teaching different ranges of pupils. Each subject has its own extensive and gradually changing literature. The following references are presented purely as an illustrative sample, based on suggestions by the author's colleagues.

They are not systematic or complete. It is essential to go hunting in libraries and bookshops to find what is best for your own needs. No sharp distinction is made between primary or middle school and secondary school requirements, although the titles themselves sometimes indicated a particular limitation of reference.

English

BRITTON, J. (ed.) (1967), *Talking and Writing, a Handbook for English Teachers*, Methuen.

CLEGG, SIR A. B. (ed.) (1965), *The Excitement of Writing*, Chatto & Windus.

HOLBROOK, D. (1961), *English for Maturity*, Cambridge University Press.

REEVES, J. (1958), *Teaching Poetry*, Heinemann.

WHITEHEAD, F. (1966), *The Disappearing Dais, A Study of the Principles and Practice of English Teaching*, Chatto & Windus.

The Use of English, a quarterly review published by Chatto & Windus.

History

BALLARD, M. (ed.) (1971), *New Movements in the Study and Teaching of History*, Temple Smith.

BURSTON, W. H. and GREEN, C. W. (ed.) (1972), *Handbook for History*

Teachers, 2nd edn, Methuen. (This is an authoritative 1088-page, £6 volume. The present reference is to Part I on The Teaching of History—17 articles in 237 pages.)

BURSTON, W. H. and THOMPSON, D. (1967), *Studies in the Nature and Teaching of History*, Routledge & Kegan Paul.

INCORPORATED ASSOCIATION OF ASSISTANT MASTERS (1965), *The Teaching of History in Secondary Schools*, 3rd edn, Cambridge University Press.

Teaching History, published twice yearly since May 1969 by the Historical Association.

Mathematics

FLETCHER, T. J. (ed.) (1965), *Some Lessons in Mathematics*, Cambridge University Press.

MATHEMATICAL ASSOCIATION (1970), *Primary Mathematics, A Further Report*, Bell.

SAWYER, W. W. (1970), *Vision in Elementary Mathematics; The Search for Pattern*; and *A Path to Modern Mathematics*, Penguin.

SERVAIS, W. and VARGA, T. (1971), *Teaching School Mathematics*, Penguin/Unesco.

WILLIAMS, E. M. and SHUARD, H. (1970), *Primary Mathematics Today*, Longmans.

Modern Languages

CALVERT, F. IRENE (1965), *French by Modern Methods in Primary and Secondary Schools*, Schofield & Sims. (A short, concise, and practical introduction.)

RIVERS, WILGA M. (1968), *Teaching Foreign-Language Skills*, University of Chicago Press. (A 403-page volume, but this reference is particularly to the 30-page chapter 1 on Objectives and Methods.)

Reading

MOYLE, D. and L. M. (1971), *Modern Innovations in the Teaching of Reading*, University of London Press.

SOUTHGATE, VERA and ROBERTS, G. R. (1970), *Reading—Which Approach?*, University of London Press.

Social Studies

LAWTON, D. *et al.* (1971), *Social Studies, 8–13*, Evans/Methuen, for the Schools Council.

Science

ASSISTANT MASTERS ASSOCIATION *et al.* (1947), *The Teaching of Science in Secondary Schools*, John Murray.

BAINBRIDGE, J. W. *et al.* (1970), *Junior Science Source Book*, Collins, for Nuffield Science Teaching Project.

EDGE, D. (1964), *Experiment, A Series of Scientific Case Histories*, B.B.C.

LAYBOURN, K. and BAILEY, C. H. (1971), *Teaching Science to the Ordinary Pupil*, 2nd edn, University of London Press.

NUFFIELD FOUNDATION (1971), *Nuffield Secondary Science, Teachers' Guide*, Longmans.

SCHOOLS COUNCIL (1970), *Changes in School Science Teaching*, Evans/Methuen.

UNESCO (1969), *New Trends in Biology*, Volume II, Unesco.

Teaching Aids

EDUCATIONAL FOUNDATION FOR VISUAL AIDS (1971), *Audio-visual Aids: Films, Filmstrips, Transparencies, Wallsheets, and Recorded Sound, Part I, Religious Education, English, Modern Languages*, EFVA. (A catalogue of resources.)

LEGGAT, R. (1970), *Showing Off, or Display Techniques for the Teacher*, National Committee for Audio-visual Aids in Education. (Simple, inexpensive, very practical.)

Bibliography

Allen, D. and **Ryan, K.** (1969), *Microteaching*, Reading, Mass.: Addison-Wesley.

Barnes, D. and **Britton, J.** (1969), *Language, the Learner and the School*, Penguin.

Beard, Ruth (1970), *Teaching and Learning in Higher Education*, Penguin.

Bishop, A. J. and **Whitfield, R. C.** (1972), *Situations in Teaching*, New York: McGraw-Hill.

Bligh, D. A. (1971), *What's the Use of Lectures?*, London University Teaching Methods Unit.

Bloom, B. S. (ed.) (1956), *Taxonomy of Educational Objectives—Handbook 1, Cognitive Domain*, Longmans.

Brown, G. A. (Autumn 1971), 'Microteaching: Innovation in Teacher Education', *Education for Teaching 86*.

Bruner, J. S. (1964, 1970), 'Some theorems on instruction', reprinted in E. Stones, *Readings in Educational Psychology*, Methuen.

Bryant, Margaret E. (24 March 1972), 'No "wild rush to the present in five instalments"—the historical world and the syllabus', *The Times Educational Supplement*.

Buist, J. (4 February 1972), 'Microteaching', *Scottish Educational Journal*.

Burgess, T. (1971), *Dear Lord James: A Critique of Teacher Education*, Penguin.

Central Advisory Council for Education (England) (1967), *Children and Their Primary Schools* (Plowden Report), H.M.S.O.

Clarizio, H. F. (1971), *Towards Positive Classroom Discipline*, John Wiley.

Clegg, Sir Alec and **Megson, Barbara** (1968), *Children in Distress*, Penguin.

Cope, Edith (1971), *School Experience in Teacher Education*, University of Bristol.

Department of Education and Science (1972), *Teacher Education and Training* (James Report), H.M.S.O.

Downes, L. W. and **Shaw, K. E.** (October 1968), 'Innovation in Teaching Practice', *Trends in Education 12*, H.M.S.O.

Duthie, J. H. (1970), *Primary School Survey: A Study of the Teacher's Day*, H.M.S.O.

Evans, K. M. (1965), *Attitudes and Interests in Education*, Routledge & Kegan Paul.

Flanders, N. (1964), 'Some relationships among teacher influence, pupil attitudes and achievement', in B. J. Biddle and W. J. Ellena, *Contemporary Research in Teacher Effectiveness*, New York; Holt, Rinehart & Winston.

Gammage, P. (1971), *Teacher and Pupil, Some Socio-Psychological Aspects*, Routledge & Kegan Paul.

Hannam, C., Smyth, P. and Stephenson, N. (1971), *Young Teachers and Reluctant Learners: An Account of the Hillview Project*, Penguin.

Hargreaves, D. H. (1972), *Interpersonal Relations and Education*, Routledge & Kegan Paul.

Haslam, K. R. (1971), *Learning in the Primary School*, Allen & Unwin.

Hilsum, S. and Cane, B. S. (1971), *The Teacher's Day*, National Foundation for Educational Research in England and Wales.

Illich, I. D. (1971), *Deschooling Society*, Calder & Boyars.

Jones, R. M. (1972), *Fantasy and Feeling in Education*, Penguin.

Kelsall, R. K. and Kelsall, H. M. (1969), *The School Teacher in England and the United States*, Pergamon.

Kemble, B. (ed.) (1971), *Fit to Teach*, Hutchinson Educational.

Krathwohl D. R. (ed.) (1964), *Taxonomy of Educational Objectives— Handbook 2, Affective Domain*, Longmans.

McAleese, W. R. and Unwin D. (1971), 'A simulated teaching environment as part of a teacher training programme,' in *Aspects of Educational Technology*, V, ed. D. Packham *et al.*, Pitman.

McFarland, H. S. N. (Autumn 1956), 'The education of James Melvill, 1556–1614', *Aberdeen University Review*.

McFarland, H. S. N. (October 1961), 'University lectures', *Universities Review*, Association of University Teachers.

McFarland, H. S. N. (February 1962), 'Education by tutorial', *Universities Review*, Association of University Teachers.

McFarland, H. S. N. (1969), *Human Learning, A Developmental Analysis*, Routledge & Kegan Paul.

McFarland, H. S. N. (1971a), 'Motivation of children's learning: the psychological aspect', The Nursery School Association of Great Britain (mimeographed).

McFarland, H. S. N. (1971b), *Psychological Theory and Educational Practice*, Routledge & Kegan Paul.

Medley, D. M., Impelletteri, J. T. and Smith L. H. (1966), *Coding Teacher Behaviors in the Classroom: A Manual for Users of OScAR 4 V*, New York: Division of Teacher Education of the City University of New York.

Midwinter, E. (1971), 'Children from another world', in *Fit to Teach*, ed. Bruce Kemble, Hutchinson Educational.

Morrison, A. and McIntyre, D. (1969), *Teachers and Teaching*, Penguin.

Neill, A. S. (1961), *Summerhill, A Radical Approach to Education*, Penguin.

Newsom, Sir J. (Chairman) (1963), *Half Our Future*, H.M.S.O.

Paulsen, F. (1906), *The German Universities*, Longmans.

Richardson, Elizabeth (1967a), *The Environment of Learning*, Nelson.

Richardson, Elizabeth (1967b), *Group Study for Teachers*, Routledge & Kegan Paul.

Richmond, W. K. (1971), *The School Curriculum*, Methuen.

Rosenshine, B. (1971), *Teaching Behaviours and Student Achievement*,

National Foundation for Educational Research in England and Wales.

Ryle, G. (1949), *The Concept of Mind*, Hutchinson.

Southgate, Vera (April 1972), 'Effective reading at every age', *Trends in Education*, H.M.S.O.

Stewart, A. (21 January 1972), 'Six golden rules for the beginner', *Scottish Educational Journal*.

Stones, E. and Morris, S. (1972), *Teaching Practice, Problems and Perspectives*, Methuen.

Sutton, C. (1971), 'Group study methods', *Education for Teaching*.

Taylor, M. T. and Sharp, R. M. (1971), 'Classroom analysis for pre-service teachers', *Education for Teaching*.

Wilson, P. S. (1971), *Interest and Discipline in Education*, Routledge & Kegan Paul.

Index

Psychology and teaching, 2
Punishment, 33, 41, 44–6
Pupil activity, 70
Pupils' names, 40

Radicalism, 15–16, 30, 37, 122
Reality, 123
Reinforcement, 42
Religious education, 120
Resources, 8, 9, 74–8
Reward, 41–3
Richardson, Elizabeth, 108
Richmond, W. K., 65, 96
Role-playing, 108
Rosenshine, B., 98
Rousseau, J.-J., 65, 78

School practice game, 23
Science and education, 125–6
Self-understanding, 35
Simulation, 83, 176
Social class, 37–8, 72, 130
Social sciences and education, 128–131
Speaking skills, 70, 72
Specialist teachers, 36
Stones, E. and Morris, S., 101
Students' double orientation, 109–113
Student-teacher status, 30
Study practice, 105
Subject skill, 28
Successful teaching, 97

Supervision, 93–4
  indirect, 90
Supervisors, 21

T-groups, 107
Teacher-centred education, 117
Teacher's day, 95–7
Teacher-education institutions, 111
Teaching
  as apprenticeship, 5
  competence, 84
  method, 78, 50
  recipes, 14, 32
  record, 28–9, 87–8
  skills, 24–30
  techniques, 15
Team teaching, 82–3, 105
Theory
  of education, 6–7, 51, 120–3
  fear of, 123–5
  meaning of, 115, 118–20
  of teaching, 50, 79, 104, 114–116
Thresholds of teaching, 17–20
Timing, 9–10, 39, 80–1
Tradition and change, 53, 122
Transitions in teaching, 39
Tutin, Dorothy, 115
Tutors, 88

Unconvincing teaching, 57

Work contracts, 42